Unlocking the Agile Mindset

The seven keys to realising Agile's full potential

By Ethann G. Castell

www.SchoolOfInnovation.net

ISBN-13: 978-0-6488075-2-0

For Mum

Table of Contents

The Agile Mindset

> The future is already here — it's just not very evenly distributed.
>
> -William Ford Gibson

Sometimes in life, we cannot know the overall effects of our actions. One small event can have vast and long-lasting ramifications. One such incident took place in February 11th 2001, when a group of software developers met at a ski lodge in Snowbird, Utah, to discuss how they could improve the way they built software.

Few who attended the gathering could have foreseen the far-reaching and enduring impact of that meeting, for it gave birth to the Agile Manifesto – a four-line description of a radical approach to solving problems - which has gone on to transform the way that the majority of digital technology is built in today's world, and is starting to define the way many businesses and other organisations work as well.

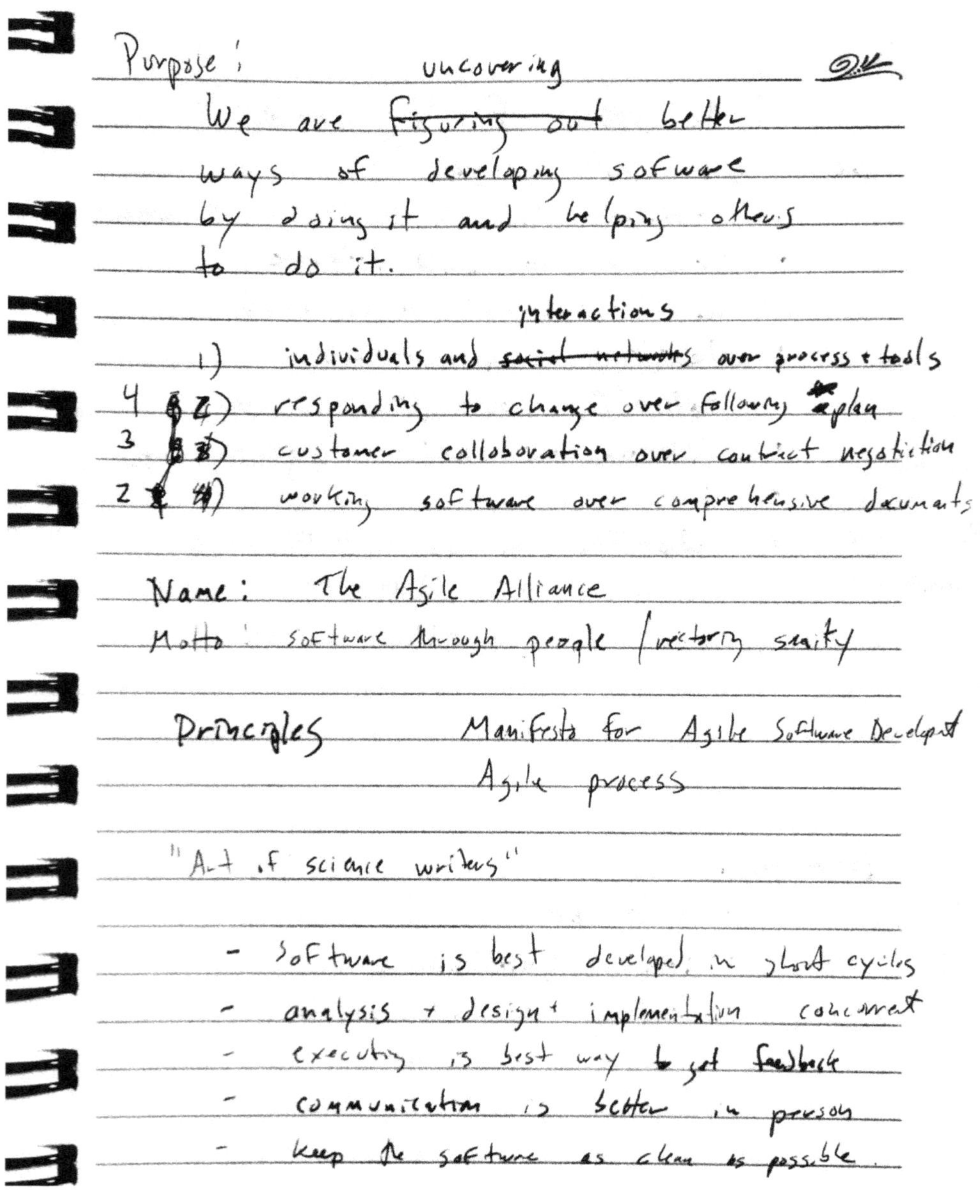

Purpose: uncovering

We are figuring ~~out~~ better
ways of developing software
by doing it and helping others
to do it.

                              interactions
    1) individuals and ~~social networks~~ over process & tools
 4 &2) responding to change over following ~~the~~ a plan
 3 &3) customer collaboration over contract negotiation
 2 &4) working software over comprehensive documents

Name: The Agile Alliance
Motto: software through people / restoring sanity

Principles   Manifesto for Agile Software Development
                         Agile process

"Art of science writers"

    - software is best developed in short cycles
    - analysis + design + implementation concurrent
    - executing is best way to get feedback
    - communication is better in person
    - keep the software as clean as possible.

Figure 1. Notes from the 2001 meeting in Snowbird. (Source: Andy Hunt)

The Agile movement seems to have taken the world by storm. From those humble beginnings on the snowfields of Utah, it has expanded beyond the realm of technology to the domains of business and government, impacting the smallest start-ups and the largest corporate giants. Agile has become so mainstream that Agile was the central theme on the cover of the May–June 2018 Issue of the Harvard Business Review (Figure 2). We have now reached the point where the term Agile is freely bandied about by politician, CEO and geek alike.

Figure 2. Harvard Business Review May-June 2018[1]

For all the hype and activity around Agile, success has still proved fleeting for many organisations. Agile has delivered amazing transformations at some organisations, more mediocre results in many others, and even a few abject failures. Often the reality has not lived up to the promise. Many have started to question whether Agile might just be another over-hyped management fad like the many that have come and gone in the past.

Myself and others have come to a different conclusion, the conclusion that Agile does in fact work very well but that most organisations have approached Agile as though it was just another process; often just a replacement for their existing Project Management framework, when in fact Agile is much more than that. Agile is a Mindset, a completely different way of thinking about the world we live in and the best way to solve problems that we encounter in that world.

Why we need another book on Agile

As has also happened to other movements which have preceded it, Agile has splintered in numerous factions, each with their own version of the right way of doing Agile, and each supported by endless amounts of training courses, certifications and high-priced consultants. This is to so-called Agile Industrial Complex – the collection of consultants and other experts who try to assert their one true way of doing Agile through their patented products and services.

This has resulted in what is commonly termed faux-Agile or Dark Agile, or as Martin Fowler (one of the creators of the Agile Manifesto) puts it:

On the surface, the world of agile software development is bright, since it is now mainstream. But the reality is troubling, because much of what is done is faux-agile, disregarding agile's values and principles.

Our challenge at the moment isn't making agile a thing that people want to do, it's dealing with what I call faux-agile: agile that's just the name, but none of the practices and values in place. Ron Jeffries often refers to it as "Dark Agile", or specifically "Dark Scrum". This is actually even worse than just pretending to do agile, it's actively using the name "agile" against the basic principles of what we were trying to do, when we talked about doing this kind of work in the late 90s and at Snowbird. (1)

Agile has become an umbrella term encompassing many different methodologies, and that the umbrella seems to be continually growing wider as more Agile derivatives continue to appear (Figure 3). This plethora of Agile methods is further muddying the waters and creating a confusing situation where two parties may be discussing Agile, but each is talking about very different things.

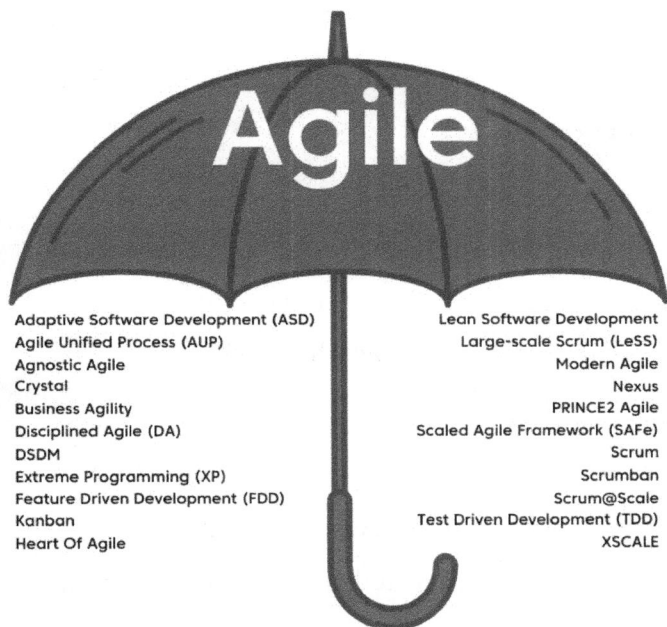

Adaptive Software Development (ASD)
Agile Unified Process (AUP)
Agnostic Agile
Crystal
Business Agility
Disciplined Agile (DA)
DSDM
Extreme Programming (XP)
Feature Driven Development (FDD)
Kanban
Heart Of Agile

Lean Software Development
Large-scale Scrum (LeSS)
Modern Agile
Nexus
PRINCE2 Agile
Scaled Agile Framework (SAFe)
Scrum
Scrumban
Scrum@Scale
Test Driven Development (TDD)
XSCALE

Figure 3. The Agile Umbrella

So what is Agile? What is it really? And why do some organisations have such success with it, while others achieve mediocre results at best? This book is about my journey to answer the fundamental that question, and the discovery of the missing key that is crucial to Agile success; the Agile Mindset.

The search for Agile

I have been blessed (or maybe cursed) most of my life with an almost insatiable curiosity. So when I got involved in Agile, it probably shouldn't have been much of a surprise that after I mastered the basics, I wanted to scratch beneath the surface to find out what made it tick. I was interested in the heated debates amongst the various Agile factions. I became curious as to what caused the differences between the Agile successes and the Agile failures, and I went on something of a mission to uncover what the underlying causes were.

Some people blamed failures on organisational culture, lack of management support, legacy processes and incompatible technology. I am sure that these contributed in part, but these causes also seemed to be the usual suspects for blaming almost any kind of failure. I wanted to know what precisely was it that contributed toward Agile success or failure?

Success leaves clues

The seeds of the answer first came to me at Scrum Australia where Forbes columnist and multiple best-selling management author, Steve Denning (at the time a director of the Scrum Alliance), gave a keynote presentation where he stated that based on his research, Agile success was almost solely based on organisations having an Agile Mindset. Perhaps even more interesting, for such organisations it didn't seem to matter which Agile methodology they implemented, be it Scrum, XP, Lean, LeSS, SAFe etc. Having the Agile Mindset was the significantly overriding success factor. Furthermore, the converse was also true, for organisations who didn't possess the Agile Mindset, it didn't seem to matter which methodology they implemented. Without the Agile Mindset, success was almost impossible.

If the seed was planted by Steve Denning, then it was germinated several months later when I attended a presentation by Stephen Townsend (Director for Network Programs for the Project Management Institute). He talked about how their research showed that Agile and non-Agile projects had similar success rates overall. When they dug deeper into Agile projects, they found one critical success factor that differentiated success and failure; The Agile Mindset.

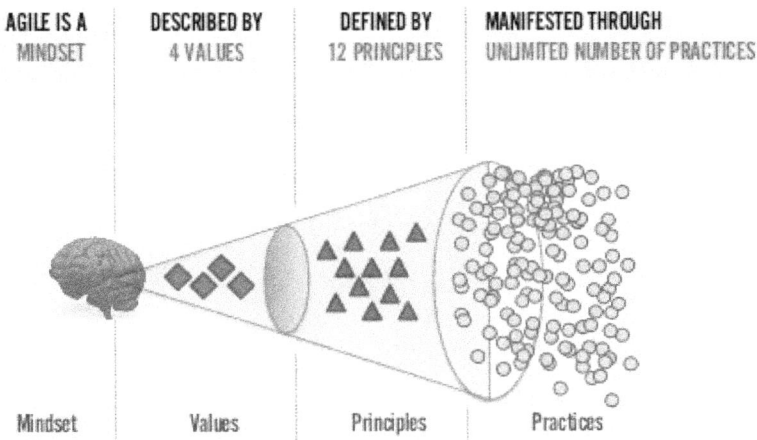

| AGILE IS A | DESCRIBED BY | DEFINED BY | MANIFESTED THROUGH |
| MINDSET | 4 VALUES | 12 PRINCIPLES | UNLIMITED NUMBER OF PRACTICES |

| Mindset | Values | Principles | Practices |

Figure 4. Agile is a Mindset[2]

If any further convincing was needed that the Agile Mindset was the key to Agile success, then it came from Dean Leffingwell, creator the Scaled Agile Framework (SAFe) whose advice the leaders who wished to transform their organisations was to first *Embrace a Lean-Agile mindset* before trying to implement any of the SAFe practices.

Why I wrote this book

Once I discovered that the Agile Mindset is the key to Agile success, I then set about trying to learn about the mindset. What was it? How was it different from other mindsets? Who could teach me about it?

Sadly, I came up mostly empty-handed. Most of the material I found in the Agile world was only concerned with a small narrow prescription of one particular process or methodology.

The material that did mention the Agile Mindset, mainly seemed to talk about it, but without providing any detail about what it actually was! Repeatedly my research and the experiences of those whom I interviewed backed up my own experience of there being a vast lack of understanding of the philosophies and principles which underlay Agile; the Agile Mindset.

Unsatisfied with what I found, I set about working to understand the Agile Mindset, digging beneath the surface layers of rhetoric and headlines to discover what was at the core of this burgeoning movement. I searched for the *why* behind the *what*; the thinking, ideas and philosophies behind the Agile practices and tools.

This book is the result of my research, and I aim to help individuals, teams and organisations fully embrace the Agile Mindset so they can realise the highest value from these new ways of working.

Supplementary Book Resources

This book has many supplementary resources - templates, guides and more – that you can download for free from www.SchoolOfInnovation.net.

Why you should care

Going through an Agile transformation typically requires a significant amount of time, effort and disruption, and at least a fair amount of discomfort and pain. Individuals and teams go through extensive education, re-education and culture change as they transition from their previous way of working to the new Agile way. If you are anything like me, then you hate wasting your time, and will want the time and effort you and your organisation invest to be rewarded. You don't want your Agile journey to have been in vain.

Many organisations move towards Agile by implementing an out-of-the-box Agile framework or methodology. Teams are trained in the processes and practices of the particular selected approach. While this may be a perfectly good starting point for some organisations, problems can arise when this is considered to be the endpoint of the transition.

Of more concern is that inevitably situations will arise which fall outside the narrow bands of the prescribed Agile method. At this point the wheels start to fall off, as without clear direction, teams do not know what to do in a particular situation. They either get paralysed and do nothing, like a deer stuck in front of headlights, or revert to their traditional way of dealing with things, often involving more documentation, more meetings and various other ways adding more bulk to the otherwise lightweight Agile processes.

Organisations and teams that go down this path often end up missing out on the benefits of Agile they had hoped to achieve. Unfortunately, some organisations fully revert to the old ways of doing things, although they may subsequently try again under new management. Yes, there are organisations which go through their second Agile transformation! Others end up working with some grotesquely mutated offspring of the Agile and traditional methods, many times providing them with the worst of both worlds.

But it doesn't have to be this way. If organisations and teams move beyond the processes and practices, they can reap the full benefits of agility. The key is to understand and embody the Agile Mindset; to move from Doing Agile to Being Agile (Figure 5).

Doing Agile	Being Agile
Fear Uncertainty	Embrace Uncertainty
Avoid Change	Welcome Change
Punish Failure	Celebrate Failure
Seldom Learning	Always Learning
People Second	People First
Limited Collaboration	Full Collaboration
Value Apathy	Value Obsession

Figure 5. Doing Agile vs Being Agile

Why you are probably only Doing Agile

There are two main reasons why many organisations are only *Doing Agile*, rather than *Being Agile*; Education and Motivation.

Education

While there is much talk about the need to move from *Doing Agile* to *Being Agile*, not many have ventured beyond these sound-bites to explore and define exactly what constitutes the Agile Mindset.

Some have grabbed hold of Stanford University psychologist Carol Dweck's Growth Mindset, and simply rebadged the *Growth Mindset* as being the *Agile Mindset*. Dweck's work describes a mindset continuum ranging from Fixed through to Growth. In a "fixed mindset" people believe their basic abilities, their intelligence, their talents, are just fixed traits. In a *growth mindset* believe that they can acquire any given ability provided they invest effort or study.

Don't misunderstand me; I am a fan of Dweck's work. However, merely having the belief that mindset change is possible through effort, does not make one Agile in the sense of being able to embrace uncertainty, deliver value or build high-performing teams. Claiming that the Agile Mindset is simply the Growth Mindset is something of a lazy approach (not by Dweck herself) and does not provide an adequate definition of all that Agile encompasses. There is a lot more to the Agile story, and the Agile Mindset, as we shall see in this book.

There seems to be a distinct lack of definition about what the Agile Mindset actually is, and it naturally follows that there is undoubtedly a lack of education about the Agile Mindset. I wrote this book to remedy this situation.

Motivation

It's likely that many people also lack the motivation to dig deep and understand the principles and philosophy underlying Agile.

Many organisations have implemented Agile without sufficiently educating their teams. I remember some years ago having a coffee with a colleague of mine, a software developer who was then working for a large multinational in Sydney, Australia. When asked how things were going at work, he replied that "Things are ok, but we have this strange new meeting where we stand up each morning, and we also have all these cards stuck to a wall. I'm not sure why we are doing this". A classic case of implementing an Agile practice without even educating the team on the process.

If people aren't even trained on a process or methodology, then I guess it shouldn't come as a big surprise that they are also not educated on the Agile Mindset underlying that process. Unfortunately, my colleague's story is not an isolated case.

My research also suggests that some organisations see Agile as merely a replacement for their current project management methodology. In a sense, they have "Implement Agile" as an item on their *To Do* list, and simply want to tick it off their list and then get back to business as usual. In such organisations there is also little motivation to dig deeper.

Andy Hunt, one of the original signatories of the Agile Manifesto and author of the bestselling book "The Pragmatic Programmer", concurs:

Agile methods ask practitioners to think, and frankly, that's a hard sell. It is far more comfortable to simply follow what rules are given and claim you're "doing it by the book." It's easy, it's safe from ridicule or recrimination; you won't get fired for it. While we might publicly decry the narrow confines of a set of rules, there is safety and comfort there. But of course, to be agile—or effective—isn't about comfort. (2)

Agile (in some variation) is so prevalent across organisations now that a large number of job advertisements require Agile. In my experience it is rare that you would find someone working in Technology that doesn't have Agile on their CV, and even less likely to find someone who would answer "No" to the question "Do you have Agile experience?". This can also cause problems because if it exerts pressure on people to say that they *know* Agile, and *are* Agile, even when this may not be the case. And it closes the door to the people who need education being able to raise their hands and ask for help, especially around the basics.

Why Be Agile?

So why should we want to *be* Agile? Isn't *doing* Agile enough? There are two key reasons why you may want to Be Agile; The Unhappy Path, and Personal Mastery.

The Unhappy Path

The *Happy Path* is a term used in Software Development to describe a scenario in which zero errors occur and no exceptional conditions arise. Consider the scenario of driving your car over to visit a friend. In the *Happy Path* scenario everything goes perfectly. The car starts the first time, there is no other traffic on the roads, every traffic light is green.... you get the picture. Many training courses, books and presentations only cover this type of *Happy Path* scenario. People are educated on how to execute under "near perfect" conditions. This is as true for Agile as it is for many other domains.

The problem of course is that unfortunately life doesn't always present us with "near perfect" conditions. In fact, in life, things rarely go exactly as planned. So in reality we will experience variations on the *Happy Path*; exceptions, errors, mistakes, miscommunications, and just plain old someone doing the wrong thing. Collectively you could call these variations the *Unhappy Path*. In our driving scenario maybe the car won't start, or you encounter a traffic jam, or your GPS guides you in the wrong direction... there are a myriad of things that could go wrong.

So how do we deal with these problems and exceptions? If we have only learned the Happy Path, then we are really only *Doing Agile*; we're equipped to execute only under near perfect conditions with minimal variations. When a significant deviation occurs, we are unsure and often unable to respond.

But when we are *Being Agile*, when we understand the underlying principles and philosophy behind Agile; the "Why" behind the doing, then we are equipped to deal with variations, any number of Unhappy Paths, because we can adjust what we are doing outside of a rote-learned process, and take effective action which is still in line with the underlying philosophy and mindset.

Personal Mastery

The second reason for wanting to Be Agile is to desire to achieve personal mastery.

Figure 6. Shu Ha Ri

Shu Ha Ri is a term used in Japanese martial arts to describe the progression from beginner to master. Martin Fowler provides the following explanation of each stage on his website.

Shu: In this beginning stage the student follows the teachings of one master precisely. He concentrates on how to do the task, without worrying too much about the underlying theory. If there are multiple variations on how to do the task, he concentrates on just the one way his master teaches him.

Ha: At this point the student begins to branch out. With the basic practices working he now starts to learn the underlying principles and theory behind the technique. He also starts learning from other masters and integrates that learning into his practice.

Ri: Now the student isn't learning from other people, but from his own practice. He creates his own approaches and adapts what he's learned to his own particular circumstances. (3)

Many people, myself included, are often not content with staying at the Shu or Ha stage. They want to achieve personal mastery and move on to Ri stage, where they can begin creating their own practice. Fully understanding and embracing the Agile Mindset can help you move to this Ri stage, where you can become an expert practitioner and should you wish, a pioneer in expanding and evolving Agile. However, we must walk before we can run, and the recommended approach is always to adopt, then adapt.

What is a Mindset?

Before we get into the details of the Agile Mindset, let's take a step back for a second and consider what actually is a Mindset? There are many definitions of what a mindset is, but one of the most succinct is as follows:

a person's way of thinking and their opinions

This is a good start, but for this book I have expanded on this simple definition to the point where I consider that a mindset encompasses the following:

- Values

- Beliefs

- Opinions

- Attitudes

- Focus (what you focus on and what you exclude)

- Mental models

- Biases

Now that we have an understanding of what constitutes a mindset, let's look at what makes up the Agile Mindset.

What is the Agile Mindset?

My research has me to conclude that the Agile Mindset covers a specific set of beliefs, attitudes and mental models which differ from other ways of thinking about work in seven key areas:

- Uncertainty
- Change lead
- Failure
- Learning
- People
- Collaboration
- Value

This book is a deep dive into each of these seven key areas, to learn how the Agile Mindset differs from traditional thinking in each area, and how you and your organization can benefit from adopting the mindset.

About this book

When putting this book together I've attempted to distil the Agile Mindset into a digestible format. Throughout the process I've tried to remain impartial in that I'm not arguing that the Agile Mindset is in any way "right" or "correct" for solving all or any specific problems. Instead I've tried to simply clarify what the Agile Mindset is, and how it contributes as the missing ingredient to Agile success, if you have decided to go down the Agile path.

Certainly previous predictive methods of getting things done (let's call them Waterfall) were also based on a set of assumptions and had their own Mindset. This Waterfall Mindset was also neither right, nor wrong, nor correct. It was simply a set of assumptions, beliefs and values about how the world worked and the best way to get things done in that world. We will see throughout this book though, the idea that the world has changed, and that the *Waterfall Mindset* is a far less appropriate approach to many of today's problems. Nevertheless, it still has its' place and purpose.

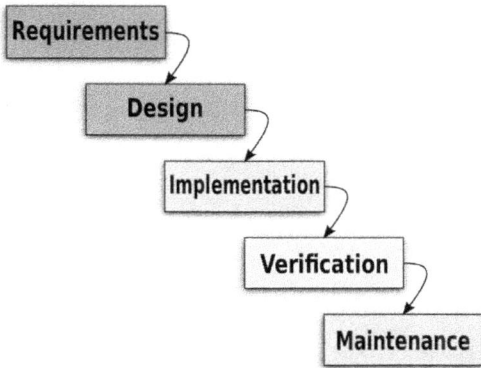

Figure 7. Typical Predictive or "Waterfall" process

I am not claiming that this book presents the complete Agile Mindset, if such a thing even exists. There are undoubtedly more, albeit likely smaller, pieces to the Agile Mindset puzzle. But I do believe that mastering these 7 keys presented here will drastically increase your understanding and mastery of Agile, and make a significantly positive impact on the outcomes you and your organisation achieve.

I use many quotes throughout this book. I find them inspirational and a very effective way of succinctly representing a complex topic in an easy-to-remember format. If you're not a fan of quotes, then all I can say is that maybe you will become one by the end of this book ☺.

Lastly, there is repetition in this book, and this is by design. The Agile Mindset is a whole that I have artificially sliced to make it easier to digest. All of the concepts are inter-related and overlap, and there will be some similarity across the discussion of topics.

Now, where did I put those keys…

Key #1. Uncertainty

> Doubt is not a pleasant condition, but certainty is absurd.
>
> -Voltaire

Uncertainty has been described as the feeling of not being sure what will happen in the future. Uncertainty often brings with it an anticipation of heightened risk and can easily cause higher levels of anxiety. This lack of confidence in our ability to predict the future ranks highly as a pain point in people's lives, and as a determinant of human behaviour.

The corollary is *certainty*; a feeling of being sure what will happen in the future. It is interesting to note that certainty is a feeling and it follows that there can often be a large disconnect between our internal feelings and the external reality. Feeling certain is not necessarily linked to a positive outcome – just visit any racetrack or casino to see this disconnect in action.

Uncertainty is an important driver of human behaviour and features in several prominent psychological and sociological models. Uncertainty features as one of the five dimensions in Geert Hofstede's widely used Cultural Dimensions framework (Figure 8), where it measures the degree that people feel threatened by ambiguous and unknown situations. Uncertainty is also one of the five determinants of human behaviour in Dr David Rock's SCARF model of communication.

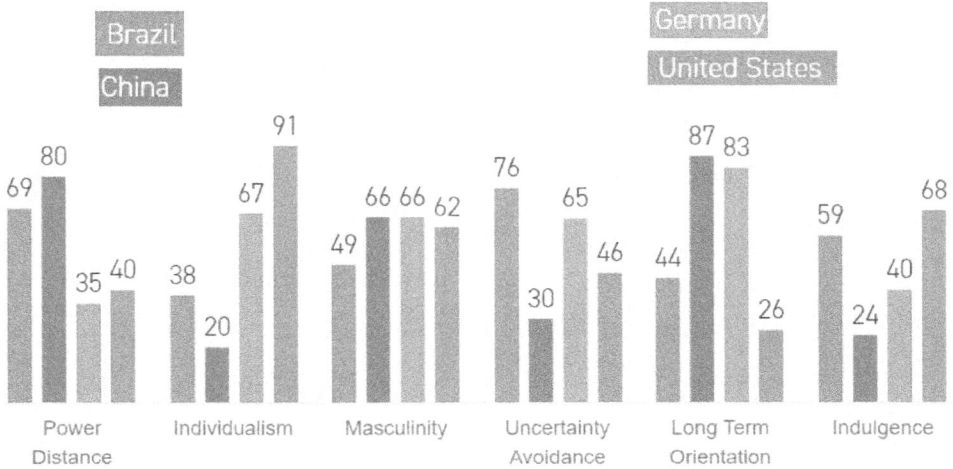

Figure 8. Comparison of 4 countries using Hofstede's model.

It seems that as human beings we crave certainty, and that we will go to great lengths to avoid uncertainty and the uncomfortable feelings associated with it. To achieve this level of comfort we tend to under-estimate the amount of uncertainty in life, and over-estimate our ability to predict the future.

Putting our denial aside, in every project or endeavour we must deal with some degree of uncertainty. Historically we have used predictive methods of managing work to provide us with a greater sense of control and certainty about the way forward. The Agile Mindset has quite a different attitude towards uncertainty and takes a different approach to dealing with uncertainty. But before we get to that, let us take a deeper look at the nature of uncertainty and visit an unfamiliar planet.

Welcome to the VUCA World

If you lived in the early 19th century, then your life was relatively simple when compared to our modern lives. Most people lived and died within close proximity to where they were born, spending their lives in much the same manner as their parents and grandparents had. In these times before the invention of the steam train, combustion engine, or even the bicycle, technology hardly changed at all. The way people went about their day-to-day business also didn't change very much either. We could postulate that outside of weather patterns, life would have seemed fairly predictable in those times.

How times have changed. The world we live in now would be unrecognisable to people from that period, not only in terms of the technological advancements we have made, but also in regards to how uncertain modern life is.

The US army noticed just how much conditions had changed even over the period from before, to after, the cold war. They identified that our ability to adapt was being outpaced by the rate of change, and created the acronym VUCA to describe the conditions in this new world.

Figure 9. VUCA

VUCA stands for Volatility, Uncertainty, Complexity and Ambiguity. Each term is defined in Table 1.

Table 1. VUCA definitions

Term	Description
Volatility	The nature and speed of the forces and catalyst behind change.
Uncertainty	The lack of unpredictability, particularly in relation to cause and effect.
Complexity	The multitude of interconnected variables affecting the situation.
Ambiguity	Unclear causal relationships and situations without precedent.

VUCA is becoming an increasingly relevant topic in strategic leadership, as organisations increasingly find that their old ways of working are not sufficient to deal with challenges of this new world.

The acknowledgement of VUCA, and a focus on developing VUCA-compatible solutions are great starting points towards mastering these challenges. But before we do, there is one major stumbling block that we must overcome, and it lies within our own heads.

Our brains don't like uncertainty

Research by de Berker et al. indicates that our brains don't like uncertainty (4). Uncertainty impairs the function of the orbital frontal cortex and this takes attention away from focusing on tasks at hand. Certainty, on the other hand, is experienced as a reward in our pattern-seeking brains through feelings such as satisfaction, stability, contentment, calmness, confidence, and comfort.

Writing for The New Yorker in *Why We Need Answers*, Maria Konnikovaput describes our need for cognitive closure.

The human mind is incredibly averse to uncertainty and ambiguity; from an early age, we respond to uncertainty or lack of clarity by spontaneously generating plausible explanations. What's more, we hold on to these invented explanations as having intrinsic value of their own. Once we have them, we don't like to let them go.

In 1972, the psychologist Jerome Kagan posited that uncertainty resolution was one of the foremost determinants of our behavior. When we can't immediately gratify our desire to know, we become highly motivated to reach a concrete explanation. That motivation, in Kagan's conception, lies at the heart of most other common motives: achievement, affiliation, power, and the like. We want to eliminate the distress of the unknown. We want, in other words, to achieve "cognitive closure." This term was coined by the social psychologist Arie Kruglanski, who eventually defined it as "individuals' desire for a firm answer to a question and an aversion toward ambiguity," a drive for certainty in the face of a less than certain world. When faced with heightened ambiguity and a lack of clear-cut answers, we need to know—and as quickly as possible. (5)

Dealing with uncertainty

Since humankind has such an aversion to uncertainty, it should come as no surprise that we have a long history of trying different approaches to deal with uncertainty. Most of the approaches have fallen into one of two camps; control or prediction.

The first set of approaches focused on trying to control situational variables through practices such as ruling with an iron first, making offerings to deities, or enforcing group conformity through social pressure and threats of punishment. The overriding belief is that if we can control enough variables then we can be certain of the outcome.

The other approaches have focused more on predicting future events. (Prediction is such a pervasive activity that I spent some considerable time deciding on whether this chapter should actually be titled Prediction. In the end I chose *Uncertainty* because I consider that *uncertainty* causes of the need for prediction). History is filled with oracles, mystics and various practitioners of divination; all who have claimed to have the power to predict the future. The underlying belief here is that if we can accurately predict the future then we can be certain of the outcome.

Writing for Psychology Today, Dr David Rock summed the up situation in his article *A Hunger for Certainty: Your brain craves certainty and avoids uncertainty like it's pain.*

There are entire industries devoted to resolving larger uncertainties: from shop-front palm readers, to the mythical "black boxes" that can supposedly predict stock trends and make investors millions. Some parts of accounting and consulting make their money by helping executives experience a perception of increasing certainty, through strategic planning and "forecasting". While the financial markets of 2008 showed once again that the future is inherently uncertain, the one thing that's certain is that people will pay lots of money to at least feel less uncertain. That's because uncertainty feels, to the brain, like a threat to your life. (6)

Friedrich Hayek, a Nobel Prize-winning economist, referred to this as the 'Pretence of Knowledge'. Hayek described the task of economics as being:

"to demonstrate to men how little they really know about what they imagine they can design."

In the real-world, both economists and market forecasters have dismal records of predicting things like recessions or major turning points in the share market. In an $80 trillion global economy driven by eight billion individual actors, divining such things is beyond the tools at our disposal (7).

So if you thought that the oracles of days past have vanished, you might be surprised to discover that they have simply taken different forms. Today's fortune-tellers now present themselves as stock-picking experts, project schedulers with 4,000 line Gantt charts and machine learning gurus with promises of soothsaying all manner of events. The Economist calls this the Perils of Prediction with the danger not being to the people making the predictions, but rather to the people who act on those predictions with certainty (8).

Is certainty real?

It seems that our brains are wired to avoid or overcome uncertainty in one way or another. And as a race, we have a long history of trying to predict and control outcomes to avoid uncertainty. But is life really that certain? Or are we just fooling ourselves?

Philosophers have been asking these questions for centuries, with perhaps the most well-known being French philosopher René Descartes who in 1637 famously deduced that outside of our own existence! Everything else must be confirmed.

From a very different field of research comes a similar conclusion. In 1927 Quantum Physicist Werner Heisenberg developed his famous Uncertainty principle, which stated that the position and the velocity of an object in the Quantum world could not both be measured exactly, at the same time, even in theory. In other words, he described the fundamental nature of the universe as inherently uncertain and that we are inherently limited in our ability to measure with precision.

Robert Burton, the author of On Being Certain, suggests that we are constantly fooling ourselves with Certainty Bias - an ungrounded sense of certainty- which is impossible to avoid.

In an interview with Scientific American, Burton responded to the question *How can people avoid the certainty bias?*

My hope is the converse; we need to recognize that the feelings of certainty and conviction are involuntary mental sensations, not logical conclusions. Intuitions, gut feelings and hunches are neither right nor wrong but tentative ideas that must then be submitted to empirical testing. If such testing isn't possible (such as in deciding whether or not to pull out of Iraq), then we must accept that any absolute stance is merely a personal vision, not a statement of fact. (9)

Uncertainty and Agile

So far we have drawn on psychology, philosophy, sociology and quantum physics to build a picture in which certainty is highly desirable from an emotional perspective, but not necessarily an accurate representation of the world. So what does this have to do with Agile and our ability to get work done?

The Project Management Institute (PMI) is an international organisation that has been codifying best practices in Project Management since 1969. They classify projects into two broad types; Predictive and Agile. For those coming from an IT background, Predictive is better known as Waterfall.

Predicative approaches are based on high levels of certainty around our ability to accurately gather requirements, predict risk, formulate accurate project plans and then to execute those plans.

The Agile Mindset embraces a different view, it sees the world as increasingly complex and inherently uncertain, and that our ability to predict and control outcomes is actually quite limited. This often raises a common barrier to adopting the Agile Mindset otherwise known as *uncertainty avoidance.*

In the case of uncertainty avoidance the fundamental issue involved is how society deals "with the fact that time runs only one way; that is we are caught in the reality of past, present and future, and we have to live with uncertainty because the future is unknown and always will be". (10)

While embracing a high level of uncertainty might cause a degree of anxiety for some, the acknowledgement of this uncertainty actually allows us to confront it and deal with it, rather than fooling ourselves that we are operating under an inflated amount of false certainty.

Admitting that we don't know everything, can't control everything, and can't predict the future very accurately, allows us the freedom to approach problems in new and effective ways. Many of these ways are otherwise known as Agile.

The Agile Mindset is not so much about giving up control as it is about giving up the *semblance* of control. In Agile, rather than relying on our ability to predict the future, we exert *control* through inspection and adaption. Adaption is such a key part of the Agile Mindset that if you are not adapting then you can argue that you are not being Agile. And here's a fun trivia fact, the original signatories of the Agile Manfesto almost chose the name *Adaptive* instead of the name *Agile*! (11)

Let's dive further into how the Agile Mindset acknowledges, approaches and deals with uncertainty.

Complexity

> Everything is simple, until you think about it.
>
> -Audrey Niffenegger, *The Time Travellers Wife*

The complexity of everyday life seems to be constantly increasing. Author and Harvard graduate Brink Lindsey described in a Psychology Today interview why he concluded that our social environments are now more complex than ever before.

Economic growth leads to greater social complexity in three main ways. First, there is more total knowledge and know-how distributed throughout the system. Second, the division of labor grows more farflung and more intricately specialized. And third, as we get richer the personal choices we face keep multiplying, from the most trivial to the most profound and life-altering. (12)

Writing in the Harvard Business Review, Columbia Business School Professor Rita Gunther McGrath noted that today's decision-makers face environments in which things that were isolated from one another just 30 years ago are bumping up against each other, often with unexpected results. That's because of a host of technological and sociological changes that occurred after 1980:

digitization of massive amounts of information,

smart systems that communicate interdependently,

the decreasing cost of computing power,

the increasing ease of communicating rich content across distances,

an increasingly wealthy human population, resulting in more participation in the formal economy, and

the wholesale rewriting of industry norms and business models. (13)

McGrath's work has a strong alignment with the concept of VUCA that was introduced earlier in this chapter. In a world where VUCA not only exists but is becoming even more prominent, how do we deal and thrive with this seemingly ever-increasing complexity?

Thankfully many smart people have spent a considerable amount of time and effort thinking about complexity and how effectively to deal with it. One of the most widely used frameworks for dealing with uncertainty and complexity, and one which fits in very nicely with the Agile Mindset, is the Cynefin Framework.

Cynefin Framework

The Cynefin Framework (Figure 10) is a conceptual framework developed in the early 2000s within IBM by Dave Snowden. Pronounced KUN-iv-in, Cynefin is a Welsh word for habitat, and has been described as a "sense-making device".

The Cynefin Framework classifies problems or situations into one of five categories (or domains) based on the relationship between cause and effect; Obvious, Complicated, Complex, Chaotic and Disorder. Based on their characteristics, problems will fall into one of the Cynefin domains, and each domain has different ways of dealing with the problems which fall within its boundaries.

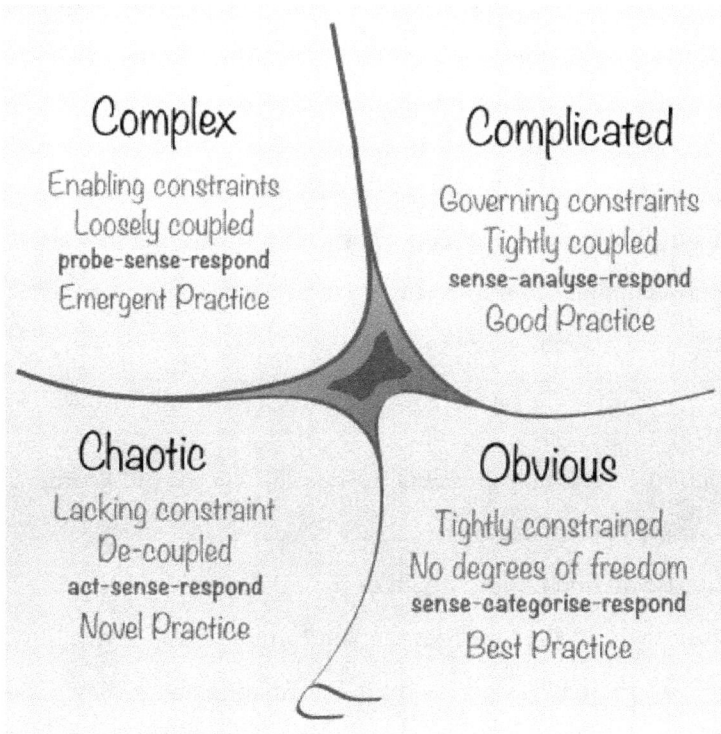

Complex

Enabling constraints
Loosely coupled
probe-sense-respond
Emergent Practice

Complicated

Governing constraints
Tightly coupled
sense-analyse-respond
Good Practice

Chaotic

Lacking constraint
De-coupled
act-sense-respond
Novel Practice

Obvious

Tightly constrained
No degrees of freedom
sense-categorise-respond
Best Practice

Figure 10. The Cynefin Framework[3]

Obvious

Obvious situations are stable and have a clear relationship between cause and effect. There is generally only one right answer and outcomes are predictable in advance; if you do X, then you should expect Y. This is the domain of "known knowns".

Complicated

Complicated situations are stable and while there is a clear relationship between cause and effect, the relationship is not self-evident and requires expertise or analysis to find the right answer. This is the domain of "known unknowns".

Complex

Complex situations have no right answers and the cause and effect relationship can only be perceived in retrospect after conducting a number of experiments. There are generally no right answers. This is the domain of "unknown unknowns".

Chaotic

Chaotic situations have no clear cause and effect. They are too confusing to wait for the results of an experiment and often immediate action needs to be taken to stabilise the system. This is the domain of unknowable.

Disorder

The shaded middle area of the diagram represents the domain known as Disorder. A Disorder situation is where you are unable to classify the cause and effect relationship. In other words you don't know which of the other domains the problem fits into. Situations within the Disorder domain cannot be dealt with directly; instead we deal with them by gathering more information about the situation or problem at hand until the point where the problem does fit into one of the other domains, and breaking down the situation into constituent parts and assign each to one of the other four domains.

Table 2 summarises the five Cynefin domains.

Table 2. The five Cynefin domains.

Domain	Cause and Effect relationship	Realm	Results	Solution	Response	Examples
Obvious	Clear and easily discernible by everyone	Known knowns	Predictable in advance	Best practice	Sense Categorise Respond	Order Processing, Compound Interest Calculation
Complicated	Not self-evident and requires analysis and the application of expert knowledge	Known unknowns	Generally predictable but only by experts	Good practice	Sense Analyse Respond	Searching for oil, car engine making noises
Complex	Can only be perceived in retrospect	Unknown unknowns	Unpredictable	Emergent solutions	Probe Sense Respond	Apollo 13, Developing a new app
Chaotic	Impossible to determine. May shift constantly or not exist at all.	Unknowables	Unpredictable	Novel solutions	Act Sense Respond	Medical Emergency, September 11.
Disorder	-	-	-	-	-	-

Cynefin and Agile

So now that you have some understanding of the Cynefin framework, how does it fit within the Agile Mindset?

The Agile Mindset makes two key assumptions in regards to complexity;

1. Agile is designed for solving complex problems.

2. Increasingly the types of problem we encounter in our modern world are complex in nature.

Agile is designed for Complex problems.

From the previous table we can see that different problems require different approaches.

Obvious and Complicated

The Obvious and Complicated domains can also be thought of as *Ordered* domains and the way to solve problems in these domains is to first sense the problem, then either categorize or analyse the problem to find the solution, and then execute the solution.

An Agile *Adapt and Inspect* experimentation cycle is not needed to solve these types of problems and while using Agile to solve these types of problems may be possible, it may actually be an inefficient (slower, more costly) way of operating. Consider a salesperson processing a sales order. They can follow the same steps they used the process the last hundred orders, rather than experimenting with new way of dealing with the problem. They have a tried and tested solution to a simple problem.

The motto for solutions to obvious problems could be "If it ain't broke, then don't fix it."

Disorder

We can also see from the table that Problems classified as Disorder as unsolvable, so therefore Agile, or any other known methodology, is not a good way to solve these types of problems.

Complex and Chaotic

This leaves us with Complex and Chaotic domains. There are similarities between these two domains in as much as they both operate in realms without any knowns. And the responses to these types of problems are quite similar.

For Complex problems we respond by Probing and Sensing, whereas for Chaotic problems we respond by Acting and Sensing. The difference between the two is that for Chaotic problems, such as a medical emergency, or a terrorist attack, we need to take immediate action, we need to do *something*, anything, to act first and then sense the results. Our first priority is to try and stabilise the system.

By contrast, in a Complex situation, such as building a new mobile app, our first response is to Probe. We form a hypothesis, conduct an experiment to probe to the system, and then sense the results of that experiment. For Complex situations we are not operating under quite the same urgency as for the Chaotic domain, so we have time to formulate our hypothesis. But as we are still dealing with unknowns we do still need to action the experiment and sense the results.

Agile is not a panacea. It is most effective and easiest to implement under conditions commonly found in software innovation: The problem to be solved is complex; solutions are initially unknown, and product requirements will most likely change; the work can be modularized; close collaboration with end-users (and rapid feedback from them) is feasible; and creative teams will typically outperform command-and-control groups. (14)

So Agile is a very good, some would say perfect, fit for dealing with Complex problems. From the perspective of the Agile Mindset, an Inspect and Adapt framework is the best way to deal to deal with Complex problems. But equally important, Agile if often not the best solution for problems which fit within the other Cynefin domains.

More problems are becoming Complex problems

The other relevant aspect of the Agile Mindset is the view that the world we live in is becoming increasingly complex; the problems we face are increasingly falling into the Complex domain, and fewer problems are falling into the Obvious or Complicated domains.

So older and more trusted methods, referred to as Best Practice or Good Practice are becoming less useful in solving modern-day challenges. Therefore, Agile is increasingly becoming the best approach for the (Complex) problems we face.

There is a very important but also quite subtle point to note here. It is not that Agile has been recently discovered or invented, and is now the solution for every problem. Rather the characteristics of the problems themselves are changing, becoming more complex and therefore better suited to an Agile solution.

We have explored how the Cynefin framework provides a way of making sense of different situations and describes an appropriate response framework for each category of situation. We have also seen that real-world situations are increasingly falling into the Complex category, and that the best response to these situations is to Probe-Sense-Respond (PSR). In the next section we will look at the thinking behind the PSR approach.

Empiricism

In theory, there is no difference between theory and practice. But, in practice, there is.

-Jan L. A. van de Snepscheut

Uncertainty often describes a situation involving ambiguous and unknown information. We saw unknowns appear earlier in the Complex and Chaotic domains of the Cynefin framework. But what is unknown information? And how do we get to "know" something; how do we turn the unknown into the known?

To find an answer, we must visit one of the major philosophical debates, a debate which has been raging amongst philosophers for centuries, and address the epistemological question of "Where does knowledge come from?"

Participants in this debate have fallen into two camps; The Empiricists and The Rationalists. You could spend a not-insignificant part of your life reading and studying the viewpoints around just this single question. For the sake of brevity, we will just take a high-level look at both schools of thought. Then we will look at how one of these two viewpoints forms the underlying philosophical basis for Agile. See if you can guess which one, and why?

But first a quick Latin lesson.

A priori and a posteriori

The Latin phrases a priori (lit. "from the earlier") and a posteriori (lit. "from the latter") are philosophical terms popularized in Critique of Pure Reason (by Immanuel Kant, published in 1781).

Figure 11. Immanuel Kant. Portrait by Johann Gottlieb Becker, 1768

A priori means that knowledge or justification is **independent of experience**

A posteriori means that knowledge or justification **depends on experience** or empirical evidence.

These terms are concerned with the relationship between knowledge acquisition and experience, and gave birth to two competing schools of thought; The Rationalists and the Empiricists. Adopting one of these viewpoints over the other can have a marked effect on how you view and interact with the world.

The Rationalist View

Rationalism distinguishes between empirical knowledge, i.e., knowledge that arises through experience, and a priori knowledge, i.e., knowledge that is prior to experience and that arises through reason. The Rationalist holds the view that knowledge can be gained by reason and intuition alone, in effect in advance of the event occurring.

The Empiricist View

The Empiricist argues that all knowledge arises through, sense perception. Thus, there is no knowledge that arises through reason alone. Empiricists share the view that there is no such thing as a priori or innate knowledge, and that instead knowledge is derived from experience (either sensed via the five senses or reasoned via the brain or mind). If we have knowledge of a subject, our knowledge is a posteriori, dependent upon sense experience.

Friends and enemies

Rationalism and empiricism do not necessarily conflict. For example, we can be rationalists in mathematics and empiricists in the physical sciences. Rationalism and empiricism only conflict when they cover the same subject area, as is the case with project work. Table 3 describes the key differences between the two approaches.

Table 3. Rationalism and Empiricism compared.

Aspect	Rationalism	Empiricism
Knowledge is derived from	Reason and logic	Experience/experimentation
Paradigm of knowledge	Mathematics	(Experimental) Science
Tool	Deductive reasoning	Inductive reasoning
Emphasis	Theory	Data
Certainty	Genuine knowledge considered to be certain.	Cannot produce certainty.
Knowledge "direction"	General to Particular	Particular to General

Famous proponents	Descartes, Spinoza Leibniz	Bacon, Locke, Hume
Project Management methodology	Waterfall	Agile

For those of you playing along at home, the answer is that Agile is based on Empiricism. Empiricism permeates throughout, and underpins much of Agile. For example, Scrum, the most widely used Agile framework, is a type of empirical process control. The difference between a defined process and an empirical process is that given the same inputs multiple times, a defined process should always produce the same output, but the same inputs applied multiple times to an empirical process could produce different outputs.

The Scientific Method

The empirical view gave birth to what we now call *the Scientific Method*. For those like me, whose last science class was quite some time ago, let's do a quick recap of the scientific method:

1. define a hypothesis

2. design an experiment that will validate or invalidate the hypothesis

3. run the experiment and gather results

4. evaluate the results

5. use newly acquired knowledge to define a new hypothesis or update the existing one

The Scientific Method is summarised in Figure 11

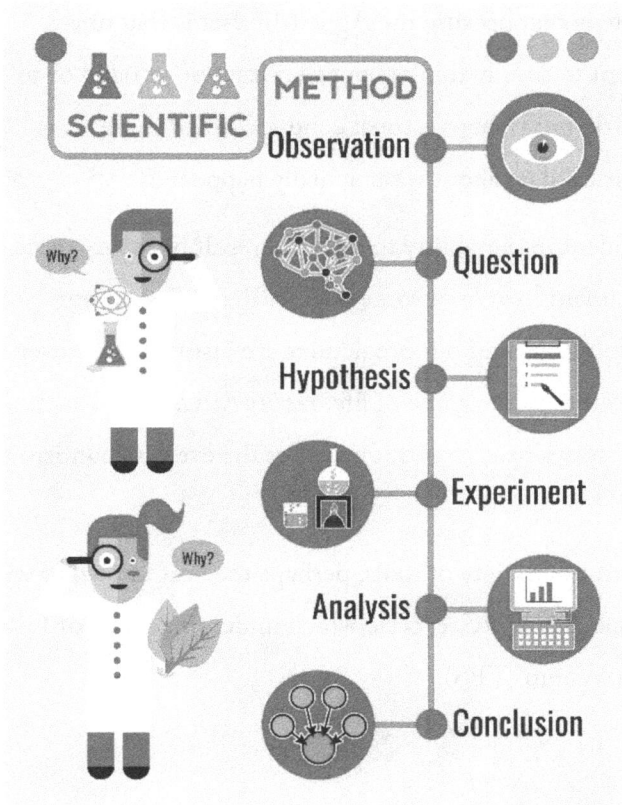

Figure 12. The Scientific Method

But what has science got to do with Agile?

You may remember that earlier we looked at the Cynefin framework and that the process to deal with Complex situations was to Probe, Sense and Respond (PSR). This PSR process **is** the scientific method. The conducting of experiments to probe the situation is a scientific approach.

The important point to note is that because the Agile Mindset is that of an Empiricist, it is not sufficient to simply think about the situation at hand or to think about what might work, but rather we must conduct one or more experiments to gather empirical data about what actually happened.

We may be extremely confident in our ability to deliver a result but every piece of work we do is still an experiment to at least some degree. Regardless of our confidence levels we need to realise that our predictions are just that, unproven predictions. It has been said that in the game of life, *reality bats last*, and as time only runs one direction we always need to wait until after the event to confirm the outcome (15).

This thinking also gave birth to a variety of tools, perhaps the best known of which is Deming's Plan-Do-Check-Act (PDCA) cycle which underpins much of Lean and the Toyota Production System (TPS).

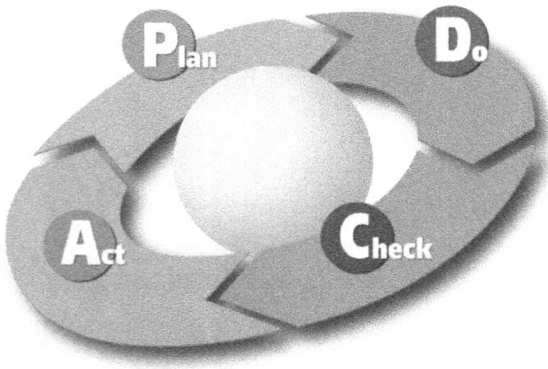

Figure 13. The Plan-Do-Check-Act Cycle[4]

PDCA is an iterative four-step management method used in business for the control and continual improvement of processes and products. Note how PDCA maps nicely with the steps of the scientific method. This is because PDCA is the scientific method in action.

Adaptive Planning

Another major difference between Agile and Predictive mindsets is in the area of planning.

Predictive, rationalist approaches, which are based on a high level of certainty in our ability to predict the future, tend to plan a long way into the future. The tool of choice is often the Gantt chart and project plans can easily contain thousands of work items (tasks) and extend years into the future. Once the plan is finalised the work is then managed to the plan. In terms of the Cynefin framework, this approach can work well for problems which fit into the Obvious domain, is less well-suited for problems in the Complicated domain and is generally not well-suited for problems in the Complex domain.

The Agile Mindset, based on the empirical Scientific Method, plans work differently using an approach known as Adaptive planning. Similar to Predictive planning, Adaptive planning also starts by defining a plan, but the difference is that Adaptive planning acknowledges that once work starts the plan will change regularly; the plan will need to be updated as we gain new knowledge.

Agile teams commonly work in iterations or Sprints, typically of two weeks in duration. At the beginning of an iteration, an Agile team plans their work for the iteration. During the iteration they attempt to complete that work. At the end of the iteration they review their work, and review the way that they worked. Then they take these learnings and plan for the next iteration. This is Adaptive planning in action; the planning for each upcoming iteration is adapted based on the outcome of the previous iteration.

The Agile Mindset views iterations or Sprints as the PDCA cycle in action, which in turn can be considered as executing the Scientific Method.

Alternatively, each iteration can also be thought of as an experiment undertaken to resolve three important questions, questions which we will explore next section.

The Sweet Spot

If we think of Agile iterations as conducting experiments to probe uncertainty, then the questions begs; what uncertainty are we testing in these experiments?

The answer is that we are testing three types uncertainty; Feasibility, Desirability and Viability, and aiming for the sweet spot in the middle which resolves all three successfully (Figure 13).

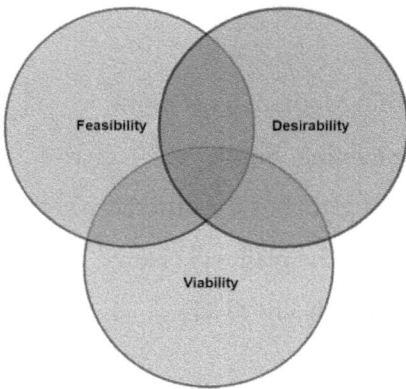

Figure 14. The Sweet Spot - the intersection of Desirability, Feasability and Viability

Feasibility, Desirability and Viability

Uncertainty is often associated with risk; while we don't know the outcome of a situation, then there is the risk that it may not turn out the way we want it to. While there are many types of uncertainty that we need to deal with in producing a product or delivering a project, the Agile Mindset condenses all these uncertainties down to three categories:

- Feasibility – can we do this?

- Desirability – will they want this?

- Viability – should we do this?

Feasibility

In many pursuits, like Software Development for example, you are almost always dealing with a degree of unknown feasibility. Many times you are trying to produce something with a high degree of uniqueness, something that hasn't been done before and with a low level of similarity to anything that has been done before. In a situation such as this, there is mostly always a degree of not knowing if what you are trying to do is actually technically possible.

Desirability

Desirability is the satisfaction of customer wants and needs. The solution may meet the specification, but does the customer actually want it? This is also known as the difference between validation and verification.

Verification and Validation

Verification and validation are two terms that are widely used but are often confused.

Verification

Verification is the process of checking that the final product meets the specification or requirements. Does the thing do what we planned it to do? Did we build it right? Is it free of defects? Most software testing, for example, covers the verification of features.

Validation

Validation on the other hand is the process of checking whether the specification captures the customer's needs. Validation is not undertaken as often as Validation. The key point here is that until you have built the product, you cannot ascertain whether the customer wants it. You may have built it to their specification, but often the customer cannot provide accurate feedback until the customer sees the product. This is why rapid prototyping approaches and small bets encourage frequent product iterations and rapid customer feedback. And this is also the basis for the Minimum Viable Product (MVP) approach which aims to produce the absolute minimum needed to validate the customers' hypothesis.

Verification and Validation sometimes get confused for one another, but Table 4 is a handy guide to the differences between the two.

Table 4. Verification and Validation compared

	Verification	Validation
Build	Did we build the thing right?	Did we build the right thing?
Goal	Free of defects.	Fit for purpose.
Test Criteria	Design Specification.	Customer or user feedback.

Viability

Whereas feasibility refers to being able to achieve a goal at any cost, viability considers whether or not we can attain the goal in an efficient manner. As an example it might be feasible to build a car that travels 5,000 kilometres to the litre. But it might cost $1 Billion to make such a car and therefore we probably wouldn't have a sustainable market for the product. So while it is feasible, it might not be viable. Often however, there is a strong link between feasibility and viability. Because we don't know if the outcome is actually possible (feasible) we also do not know what the finished solution will be, nor what it will be composed of, so we are often unable to assess the viability until we have a feasible solution.

These three categories represent the three areas of uncertainty that we must always deal with in building a new product or solving a problem. Building on the empirical approach described earlier, every experiment should aim to answer one or more of these three questions, to reduce one or more of these uncertainties.

If our product hits the sweet spot, the overlapping area in the middle of the Venn diagram, where the uncertainties on all three dimensions are lowest, we have a solution that we can and should build, and that customers love. This is the target area that we are constantly aiming for in Agile.

Summary

The Agile Mindset sees most situations as inherently uncertain, and that the best way to deal with this uncertainty is to take an empirical approach of experimentation and constant inspection and adaption. The uncertainty faced falls into three categories; feasibility, viability and desirability. Every experiment we do should aim to reduce the uncertainty in one or more of these areas and head towards the sweet spot where we can and should build something, which also delights our customer.

Key Points

- We now live in a VUCA world.
- Our brains avoid the pain of uncertainty and crave the rewards of certainty. Our brains will go to quite some lengths to promote the illusion of certainty.
- The Cynefin framework provides a powerful way of categorizing the level of uncertainty for a situation.
- Agile is best suited for solving Complex problems.
- Problems are increasingly becoming Complex in nature.
- Agile is based on the empirical scientific method where we use Inspection and Adaption to deal uncertainty rather than using prediction.
- Agile iterations are Plan-Do-Check-Act (PDCA) cycles which are effectively scientific experiments.
- Agile planning is adaptive and based on empirical inputs.
- There are three types of uncertainty we need to resolve for simultaneously:
  - Feasibility

- ○ Viability

- ○ Desirability

Remember to get this book's free supplementary resources from www.SchoolOfInnovation.net.

Key #2. Change

It is not necessary to change. Survival is not mandatory.

W. Edwards Deming

It is often said that *change is the only constant*. While this is a clever play on words, it also contains more than a small grain of truth within. In a VUCA world that is inherently uncertain and unpredictable, as we described in the previous chapter, things will change, and change often.

But if change is so prevalent then why do people seem so resistant to change, and why have many traditional management methods seemingly been resistant to change?

Part of the reason for the resistance to change is undoubtedly that change means going from a known situation to a relatively unknown situation. The unknown generally carries a higher degree of uncertainty and risk than the known. In most endeavours in life we want to limit our risks so therefore it follows that we would also want to minimize the amount of change.

Traditional (predictive) ways of working have tended not to be very change-friendly. They typically included an expectation that once requirements have been defined (generally upfront) that little should change from that point onwards. Change was generally not expected or welcomed.

The Agile Mindset has a very different perspective on change. It sees change as a very normal occurrence and one that can bring new opportunities and new possibilities. It expects changes to occur and to occur constantly, whether it is to requirements, the internal environment, the external environment or even to the way a team works together. But the Agile Mindset goes further than just expecting change, and as we will see in this chapter, the Agile Mindset doesn't just expect change, it welcomes change and actively engages with change!

Expect Change

> If the rate of change on the outside exceeds the rate of change on the inside, then the end is near.
>
> Jack Welch, CEO of GE

In our modern lives, change is constant. To get a perspective on how much quickly life is changing, let's look at just a few of the new technologies introduced between 2000 and 2010.

- AirBNB (2008)
- Android (2003)
- Apple iPod (2001)
- Facebook (2004)
- Firefox Browser (2005)
- Fitbit (2009)
- Gmail (2004)
- Google Chrome (2008)
- Google Maps (2005)
- Instagram (2010)

- iPad (2010)
- iPhone (2007)
- Kindle (2007)
- Minecraft (2007)
- Reddit (2005)
- Twitter (2006)
- World of Warcraft (2004)
- YouTube (2005)

These technologies have transformed our lives. And this is only the change from one decade!

Why should we expect more change and what are the benefits of doing so?

Expecting change means that we are dealing with the reality of a changing environment, seeing with our eyes wide open and therefore having the opportunity to acknowledge and work with the change rather than being the victim of change.

Many of the reasons to expect change relate to the external environment – the environment that our organisations operate within. Although we might not like to admit it, we often have little control over this external environment, but changes to the external environment can have significant impacts on our internal environment.

In his book The Innovation Master Plan, Langdon Morris identifies six major forces that are driving the changes which are occurring across much of today's world.

- Commoditization
- The digital revolution
- Social mediaization

- Globalization

- The turbulent world

- Acceleration (or running faster to stay in the same place) (16)

We could easily add more items, or variations of the existing items, to this list. However, as it stands this is a good starting point for assessing the changes taking place in our world. Let's take a look at each force in a little more detail.

Commoditization

Commoditization is the processes by which goods that have economic value and are distinguishable in terms of attributes (uniqueness or brand) end up becoming simple commodities in the eyes of the market or consumers. (17)

Commoditization of technology can be an especially powerful enabler of change. Cloud CRM (Customer Relationship Management) software provider Salesforce is a great example of this type of technological commoditization and the impact it can have. Before Salesforce, only large organizations could afford top-end CRM systems and the capabilities that these provided. Therefore, larger organisations with bigger budgets could gain advantages from this technology that over smaller organizations with their smaller budgets could never afford.

But Salesforce commoditized CRM, they produced a cloud-based pay-per-user model, meaning that a small organization could purchase just a few licenses but have access to exactly the same functionality as larger organisations which produced

The change to commoditization CRM provided a new opportunity for smaller CRM customers, but it was highly disruptive to companies who produced CRM software and required them to also adapt to the changing environment.

The digital revolution

The McKinsey and Company report *The four global forces breaking all the trends* describes the breadth and pace of the digital revolution.

Technology—from the printing press to the steam engine and the Internet—has always been a great force in overturning the status quo. The difference today is the sheer ubiquity of technology in our lives and the speed of change. It took more than 50 years after the telephone was invented until half of American homes had one. It took radio 38 years to attract 50 million listeners. But Facebook attracted 6 million users in its first year and that number multiplied 100 times over the next five years. China's mobile text- and voice-messaging service WeChat has 300 million users, more than the entire adult population of the United States. Accelerated adoption invites accelerated innovation. In 2009, two years after the iPhone's launch, developers had created around 150,000 applications. By 2014, that number had hit 1.2 million, and users had downloaded more than 75 billion total apps, more than ten for every person on the planet. As fast as innovation has multiplied and spread in recent years, it is poised to change and grow at an exponential speed beyond the power of human intuition to anticipate. (18)

Social mediaisation

Social media has transformed the world and had a marked effect on individual behaviour. Viral memes can spread across the globe at incredible speeds potentially rocketing your organisation to global stardom, or just as easily condemning it to ruin.

Three billion people, around 40% of the world's population, use online social media – and we're spending an average of two hours every day sharing, liking, tweeting and updating on these platforms, according to some reports. That breaks down to around half a million tweets and Snapchat photos shared every minute. (19)

Globalization

If the digitisation, commoditization and social media hadn't changed the landscape enough, globalisation has exerted even more pressure on organisations to adapt and change.

Globalisation is the process by which the world is becoming increasingly interconnected as a result of massively increased trade and cultural exchange. This interconnectedness amongst humans on the planet is sometimes also referred to as the 'global village' where the barriers of national and international boundaries become less relevant and the world, figuratively, a smaller place

Thomas L. Friedman 's international best-selling book The World Is Flat: A Brief History of the Twenty-first Century analysed the globalization phenomenon and coined the phrase *you can innovate without having to emigrate.* The book title is a metaphor for viewing the world as a level playing between industrial and emerging market countries. The corner store in the west of Scotland is now competing with Amazon.com and the software developer in New York is now competing against the software developer in Ukraine.

The turbulent world

Anecdotally the world seems to be becoming increasingly turbulent. On his blog at innovationmanagement.se Langdon Morris writes:

I picked a day at random, November 26, 2010, and that day's news from across the globe included: gang violence in Rio de Janeiro, drug violence in Colombia and Mexico, students protesting education cuts in Italy, social services cuts in Greece and Ireland due government debt crises, as well as political or territorial disputes between India and Pakistan, North and South Korea, Israel and the Palestinians, and Japan and China. That's not a complete list of the world's troubled spots, but it's enough to remind us just how widespread the turbulence is.

And then a few days later, WikiLeaks began releasing a set of 250,000 diplomatic cables, an action that some claimed was the beginning of a real "cyber war." And a few days after that, the government of Ukraine announced that they would soon be offering tours of the Chernobyl nuclear reactor site. (16)

Acceleration (or running faster to stay in the same place)

Each of the previous five forces on their own can present a significant amount of change that individuals and organizations need to deal with. But these forces are not occurring independently of each other, rather they are combining and working together to amplify the rate and impact of change.

Morris writes:

As their impacts converge, the result is the potential for thoroughly disruptive acceleration and the amplification of their impact in a way that is decisive and inescapable. (16)

So what does this all this external change mean for Agile and the Agile Mindset?

It means that organisations are now operating in hyper-competitive and rapidly changing markets. They need to expect external change to occur and align to be more responsive and able to adapt to change, and to take advantage of new opportunities much better than they have in the past. In other words, they need to be more Agile.

Internal change

Changes to the external environment directly influence the internals of our organisations. When the competitive landscape changes we need to be ready and able to respond in a timely matter. As W. Edwards Deming said in his quote at the beginning of this chapter, survival is not mandatory. Organisations that can't or won't change risk not surviving at all. For most organisations there is no implicit safety net that will guarantee their survival, even though they may think and act otherwise.

In such an environment it should come as no surprise that requirements will change, and change quickly, and we should expect such change. Whereas traditional work methods have been less than change-friendly, the Agile Manifesto says to expect change through its second principle:

Welcome changing requirements, even late in development. Agile processes harness change for the customer's competitive advantage.

The Cost of Change is changing

One particular factor that allows for rapid internal change is that the *cost of change* has traditionally been high, especially where technology has been concerned. But prices of technology have changed dramatically, and so have many of the associated costs of change. The following table contains some examples of how the cost of technology has reduced dramatically over the past few decades.

Table 5. Reduction in computer hardware costs over four decades.

Item	Comparison year	Cost	Base year	Cost	Cost reduction %
Computer hard drive storage	2016	$0.033 / GB	1981	$340,000.00 per GB	99.99%
Computer memory	2017	$0.0071/Mbyte	1981	$8,800/Mbyte	99.99%
Computer processors (CPU)	2017	$0.03 per GFLOPS	1984	$18,750,000 per GFLOPS	99.99%

Why is the cost of change important?

Because the higher the cost of change, the more likely you are to want to avoid change. If the cost of change is high, then it may make economic sense to spend a lot of time in upfront planning and design because this may be cheaper than making costly changes later on. However, at some point we are likely to encounter the point of diminishing marginal returns, the point where were the benefits of extra planning and design start to diminish relative to their cost. At a certain point, you have to be ready to take a leap of faith and explore a potential possibility. (20)

If our cost of change is low, then it no longer makes the same sense to spend so much time in upfront planning and design. With a lower cost of change it may be more economical and more effective to build something, for example, a Minimum Viable Product (MVP), and then make incremental modifications until we have exactly what we want.

In Agile projects we tend to follow this method of making lots of small incremental changes and getting rapid feedback from stakeholders and customers who are heavily engaged throughout the development process.

Feedback Loops

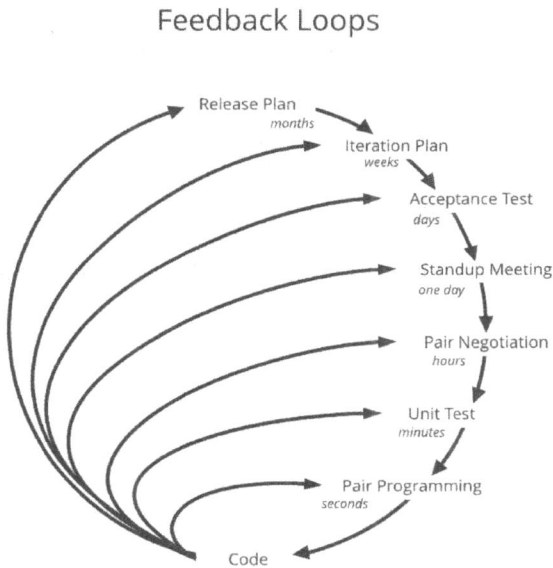

Figure 15. Feedback Loops. [5]

A useful perspective on contemplating Agile as a whole, is to picture the whole process as a series of nested feedback loops (Figure 14) where we are constantly gathering feedback at multiple levels, and continually adapting and responding to that feedback.

Of course, the more we open up to feedback, the more requests for change we must expect to occur.

What to do when we expect change?

We have looked at a large number of external and internal factors driving change and highlighted that in this environment we should expect things to change often and continually. Change largely becomes a matter of *when*, rather than *if*.

What type of mindset do we need to have in order to work effectively while continually expecting change? The stoic philosopher Epictetus provides us with a good starting point in Discourses, 2.5.4–5.

The chief task in life is simply this: to identify and separate matters so that I can say clearly to myself which are externals not under my control, and which have to do with the choices I actually control.

Epictetus' sentiments are also echoed in the famous Serenity Prayer.

God grant me the serenity to accept the things I cannot change, courage to change the things I can, and wisdom to know the difference.

The wisdom of these quotes is that they guide us to focus mainly on those things that we can control; also known in psychology as our *locus of control*. We should not ignore those things that we cannot control, just like we should not ignore the weather, but the majority of our focus needs to be on the things that we do have some agency over. From this we can formulate a simple strategy (Table 6) for dealing with change that we expect to occur continually:

- Act on the change that is within our control.

- Monitor change that is outside of our control.

Table 6. Strategy for response to change

Change	Strategy
Within our control	Act
Outside our control	Monitor

Welcome Change

> He who rejects change is the architect of decay.
>
> -Harold Wilson

Traditional predictive project approaches would often attempt to gather all requirements upfront. Customers had one chance to state all of their requirements, and it was made painfully clear to customers that any changes after the start of the project would require a dreaded *Change Request*, which more often than not would result in high additional cost. In this type of scenario change was seen as the enemy at worst, and an annoyance at best.

The Agile Mindset takes a different approach and welcomes changing requirements, which is why the second principle of the Agile Manifesto reads:

Welcome changing requirements, even late in development. Agile processes harness change for the customer's competitive advantage. (21)

In Agile we tend to constantly re-prioritise our work backlog. We do this because relevance and priority fluctuate. In the face of uncertainty and constant change, the must-have item that was critically important one month ago may now become a nice-to-have or even no longer required. Embracing this fluctuating relevance means that we don't become too attached to what is in our future pipeline of work. We recognise and understand that the future workload is always subject to change. This is also the reason that we don't spend much time defining requirements which are too far out in the future.

Let's now take a look at why we should welcome change and the benefits of doing so.

Embrace change

Kent Beck's book Extreme Programming Explained is one of the landmark Agile writings. The subtitle of the book is *Embrace Change* and I believe that Kent chose this subtitle for a very specific reason; I think he wanted to highlight that we are change-resistant by our very nature and therefore we need to work hard to make ourselves embrace change and all the uncertainty, disruption, fear and anxiety that comes with it.

If we decide not to embrace change then our only other options are to resist or ignore the change. History would suggest that either of these approaches is fraught with danger. Consider the courier company that decided to resist the move from horses to motor-powered vehicles, or the corporate who decided to resist computers and email in lieu of remaining with typewriters and faxes. Neither of these companies would survive very long as the advantages their competitors would gain from embracing new technology would put them out of business.

Change is good

To improve is to change; to be perfect is to change often.

-Winston Churchill

The need to embrace change was highlighted well by the popularity of the business fable *Who Moved My Cheese? An Amazing Way to Deal with Change in Your Work and in Your Life*. Published in 1998 the book became a mainstay in many organisations where it was used to prime employees about upcoming change the how to deal with it.

The fable tells the story of two mice who live in a maze but encounter major changes when the cheese that has always been in one fixed location, is no longer there. Faced with uncertainty and possible starvation, the mice make two very different choices. One mouse decides to resist the change and wait for the old cheese to return to the same location. The other mouse embraces the change and starts searching the maze for new cheese.

As you might have already guessed, the first mouse almost dies of starvation, while the second mouse finds new cheesy riches. While maybe a tad patronizing, the book highlights the important point that change always brings new opportunities and that the only things stopping us from seeing and embracing those new opportunities is a shift in mindset.

Rather than change being seen as an annoyance or some sort of enemy, change should be seen as a good thing. Why? Because change brings new opportunities to explore and capitalize upon.

Invite change

If we have embraced that idea of constant and rapid change, and can now see that this change is actually a good thing, then the next step is to go ahead and actually invite change.

In traditional predictive projects we have tended to get the customer involved in the beginning at the scoping and requirements gathering stages, and then not again until much later in the project. At this later stage of the project, changes are generally not welcome and often costly to implement.

In Agile we regularly invite changes, both to the product and to the process; the way the team works together and with stakeholders. At the end of every iteration most teams will showcase their work to their product owner and importantly, invite feedback on what they have delivered.

Verification and Validation

Most work processes include a verification step, the point where we compare the outcome we produced, with the specification of what we wanted to produce. However, historically we have been concerned with validation – the checking that the specification actually meets the customer's needs. So while we can verify that we *built it right*, we don't so often validate that we *build the right thing*.

With an Agile Mindset our goal is always to produce the highest possible customer value. If we have built an increment of a product and the product owner or customer wants further changes then rather viewing this as a failure, we should view it as a normal part of the ongoing discovery process, a successful step towards delivering what the customer really wants. Because although we would like our customers to be able to tell us exactly what they want upfront, in reality they are often unable to do this. Even when they can provide a detailed description of what they want, it is often not until they get the first version in their hands to touch, taste and test, that they discover what they *really* want or need. This should not necessarily be viewed as a failure of gathering requirements but rather as a natural step in the discovery process towards delivering customer value. From the customer's perspective, it is sometimes a case of IKIWISI (I'll Know It When I See It).

We saw earlier Deming's Plan-Do-Check-Act (PDCA) cycle and how many Agile practices can be viewed as variations on this cycle. At the Check stage we are actually opening up to change, inviting change into our process. At this point we have tried to build what we understood the customer wanted and now we need to verify that we have built what we wanted to build, and importantly validate that this actually meets the customer needs. This is the point where we invite the customer to say "that is what I said I wanted, but now that I've seen what you're delivered I can actually see more clearly what is really needed".

This approach is not some new invention or discovery, it has appeared in approaches such as rapid prototyping and incremental development. However, what is relatively new is the acknowledgement and recognition that the customer will not always know what they really want or need, and that the customer and the team need to work collaboratively to discover the right solution together.

Be Change

If we have grown to expect change and then to welcome it, in a very Shu-Ha-Ri way, the final stage is to progress to where we become change.

Atlassian is a well-known software company who make a number of popular tools including the popular Agile tool JIRA. The company is an impressive success story. Founded by two young Australian entrepreneurs on a credit card in 2002, the company has grown to over 2000 employees worldwide and over $US 800 million in revenue. Interestingly the company is based on five simple core values:

- Open company, no bullshit

- Build with heart and balance

- Don't #### the customer

- Play as a team

- **Be the change you seek** (22)

All of these values are deceptively simple, yet very powerful. The last of Atlassian's five values is the one I want to draw your attention to here.

When I spoke with people at Atlassian this value came through loud and clear in their communication. Inside the company, there is a clear ethos of taking ownership for the change you want. In other words, don't say how you want things to be, take action and make them the way you want them to be.

What is especially interesting about Atlassian, is that these values are not aspirational, they aren't attributes Atlassian expects its employees to grow into. Instead, they are attributes Atlassian makes sure its potential employees fit into, **before** hiring them. (23)

How is this attitude different from the standard Agile practised in many organisations? Consider the Retrospectives that many teams hold at the end of an iteration. Often these solicit feedback on the previous iteration into a framework such as Good, Bad, Better or Start, Stop, Continue. The Better or Start categories represent actions that should be put in place to improve how the team works in the future. But coming up with the ideas is much easier than actually implementing them. And similar to the concept of work only being of value when it is Done, an idea for improvement only has value once it has been put into action.

Inside Atlassian, and from the Agile Mindset perspective, we need to be the change that we seek. Instead of simply putting forward an idea for change, we should take action and champion the change.

The Art of the Possible

Ken Schwaber, the co-creator of Scrum along with Jeff Sutherland, often describes Scrum as the *Art of the Possible*.

On a personal note, this is the one phrase that got me hooked on Agile and has become something of a mantra for me ever since, not just in my work life but also in my personal life. To me, it blends the best of positive psychology and the growth mindset with stoic philosophy to produce a worldview that allows for optimism but very much remains grounded in pragmatic reality.

Quite simply, this statement means to **do the best we can with what we have at the time**. This is such a simple statement that it is easy to overlook the power within it.

Breaking it down, firstly we can only ever work with what we have, we can't work with things or people that we don't have available to us. We must deal with the situation at hand how it is and not how we want it to be, or how we might think it should be. We need to face things as they are rather than blaming others because they are not as they should be.

Secondly, we can only ever do the best we can. We can't expect to do better than our best, because if we could do better, then we are not doing our best. We can't expect a team to do one month's work in one week, no matter how much we want it or how urgent it is. We can't expect all our software developers to all be as brilliant as the scientists working on Artificial Intelligence (AI) in the labs at Google and IBM. And we can't expect people with a few weeks' experience to perform at the same level as people with several years of experience.

Why is this so important? Because in life we seldom have the resources, people, time, money, clearly defined requirements, stable environments and un-competitive competitors that would be ideal. But we often put off taking action until conditions are perfect. We must avoid this type of pursuit of perfection.

The Art of the Possible means doing what we can right now. Rather than succumbing to the noise surrounding the problem and what can't be done, a team's energy is best directed toward solving the problem with the available resources and focusing on what can be done.

Breaking through Impossible

Embracing the Art of the Possible, also means resisting the urge to label a situation as impossible. Labelling situations as impossible is often taking the easy way out. For example, we can't do anything because we are relying on XYZ team.

In his book Agile Project Management with Scrum, Ken Schwaber tells the story of a team he was a Scrum Master on, a team where a developer completed their work mid-sprint as agreed and then went hiking in Yellowstone National Park for two weeks (where he was unreachable). As Murphy's Law would have it, three days after the developer went on vacation his code broke and the team was unable to continue progressing towards their Sprint goal. Rather than taking the easy way out and labelling the situation as impossible, Ken embraced the Art of the Possible, went out and hired an ex-FBI Private Investigator (PI) to find the developer. The PI was able to locate the developer within two days, the developer was able to assist the team, and the Sprint goal was achieved by the team. (24)

Many people would say that this is an extreme measure. And I would largely agree with them. From Ken's point of view, he came up with an innovative, if not unconventional, way to remove the impediment at a minimal cost. While I am not suggesting that you go to the same lengths as Ken, what I am suggesting is that impossible is often only an artificial barrier.

There are many ways to break through this barrier and whole books have been written on the subject. A good place to start is with The Power of Impossible Thinking by Colin Crook, E Gunther Robert, and Yoram Wind, which describes in some details how to transform mental models to your advantage. (25)

You can start your journey beyond the impossible by asking a few pertinent questions such as these six problem-solving questions:

1. Who else could overcome this problem and how would they do it?

2. What would we do if we could not fail?

3. How would we approach this if we had unlimited time, budget and resources?

4. Who needs to change in order for us to solve this problem?

5. What would \<expert\> do in this situation?

    a) (Use a relevant expert, maybe someone like Steve Jobs, Jack Welsh or Nelson Mandella)

6. What would happen if we did nothing?

What to change

We have embraced and welcomed change, and reached the point where we want to actively be the cause of change and overcome the impossible. So what do we go out and change? The Agile Mindset focuses on change in three areas:

- Product
- Process
- People

We will now take a look at each of these three areas in more detail.

Product

The product is the goal we are trying to achieve, the outcome that we are working to achieve, or the product that we are trying to produce. Most people are familiar with change in this area when customer requirements change, and the product must change to meet these changed requirements. As we have already seen, within under the Agile Mindset we expect and invite this product change through both verification and validation.

Process

Process refers to the actions we take to achieve the goal. In Agile in addition to inspecting and adapting the product on a regular basis, we also inspect and adapt our processes on a regular basis. In the Scrum world, process inspection takes place regularly in a meeting called a Retrospective.

Retrospectives can be considered to be an implementation of Donald Schön's reflection-on-action in which we periodically and continually reflect on our previous actions as a path to developing wisdom (26). During a Retrospective, the team will review how they have worked together over the iteration and look for ways to improve their processes.

Retrospectives are such an important part of the Agile Mindset because they acknowledge that things can and do continually change, and that the way the team has worked up until now may no longer be the best way to continue.

People

Working on teams and with customers can be challenging and as much as we might like to at times, we generally cannot change the actual people we are working with. But if we focus on what is within our locus of control, we can change and improve our interactions with people by employing our Emotional Intelligence (EQ) to increase our understanding and empathy for the people we are working with. We can work on creating greater psychological safety within our teams. We can try new ways of interacting with people and improve our relationships and the way we collaborate.

When to change

The short answer is **often.**

Change should not be thought of a one-off activity, or considered irregular in any way. Our goal is to embrace the Japanese concept of Kaizen, and seek continuous ongoing improvement indefinitely.

When we build inspection and adaption into our product, process and people, incremental change becomes a normalised way of working within our organisations.

Summary

Humans are typically change-resistant and for good reason; change is almost always accompanied by the fear of the unknown, rather than the relative safety of the status quo.

We have looked at how much change is taking place in the VUCA world that we now live in, and how this external change requires a similar amount of internal change. So to a large degree, both at an individual and organisational level, we have to change simply in order to survive.

Beyond accepting change, we looked at how the Agile Mindset welcomes change, it embraces change and invites change. We looked at the benefits of adopting this aspect of the Agile Mindset.

Lastly we saw how we could move into a state of "being change", where our approach is to take personal responsibility for making change, focusing on what is possible in any situation, and constantly seeking to make small incremental changes.

Keys Points

- The VUCA world is changing at an increasing rate, meaning that in an increasing number of industries, change is necessary for survival.

- Agile can be thought as a series of nested feedback loops where we continually gather feedback (inspect) and then adapt based on this feedback.

- Change should be expected, welcomed and embraced.

- Agile involves a continual discovery process where the customer seldom knows what they want or need up front. Often we need to reply on IKIWISI (I'll Know It When I see It).

- In order to make things happen we must take responsibility and *be the change we seek in the world.*

- Focus on what can be done with *The Art of the Possible* and challenge impossible thinking.

Download your free supplementary resources from www.SchoolOfInnovation.net.

Key #3. Failure

Success consists of going from failure to failure without loss of enthusiasm.

-Winston Churchill

We have looked at how the Agile Mindset views the world as uncertain, complex and continually changing, and suggested that our individual and organisational response to these conditions should be to embrace and welcome change. But if we make many changes then undoubtedly not all changes will be successful, there be successes and failures in the changes we make. And this brings us to the highly-emotive subject of failure. But first, a few questions.

Why do we have projects manager on projects? Think about it for a minute. Surely once we have defined all the work tasks, then we only need a good planner to schedule all those tasks and then they will take care of themselves?

A similar question is asking why do we have a Check stage in the Plan-Do-Check-Act cycle? Why not just Plan-Do-Act or even just Plan-Do?

The answers to these questions are because things often don't go to plan. We can have all manner of unforeseen events derail our intentions, and even in perfect conditions, sometimes our ability to execute can let us down. This lack of success is otherwise known as failure.

Failure. What a highly emotive word. Just the mention of the word can make people uncomfortable. It has been suggested that *fear of failure* is a leading cause of organizational dysfunction (27). A google search for "fear of failure" results in over 179 million results. The prevalence of this fear goes a long way to explaining why traditional methods such as Waterfall have focused so much on *getting it right the first time* through exhaustive efforts such as Big Design Up Front (BDUF).

This fear of failure is common to most of us, at least to some degree, that we develop tendencies to either avoid failure (by not trying something new) or to cover up our mistakes. The Agile Mindset takes a refreshingly different approach to failure. It sees failure as commonplace, a naturally occurring event. Certainly failure is not our goal - we don't start something with an intention not to succeed, but we also don't deny or hide from failure.

In my personal experience, this is the most difficult part of the Agile Mindset for people and organizations to adopt, but also potentially the most rewarding.

Failure is more than an option

> Failure is only the opportunity to begin again more intelligently.
>
> -Henry Ford

If you have ever seen a motivation speaker in action, then the chances are that you have heard the phrase "Failure is not an option". It is often attributed to NASA Flight Director Gene Kranz, as the core of his directive to the Apollo 13 ground team, when they were working feverously to find a way to get astronauts home alive in their malfunctioning spacecraft.

In a life and death situation as with Apollo 11, such a mindset is admirable and maybe even quite necessary to maintain focus and motivation. But the work that most of us do is more mundane, or at least failure doesn't result in loss of life. So for the rest of us, does failure actually become an option? The Agile Mindset, as we shall see, views failure as actually more than an option, and almost as a necessity.

Failure is often necessary

Sir Ken Robinson made one of the most viewed TED talks ever, titled *Do schools kill creativity?* During his presentation he talks about how our education systems focus too much on getting the correct answer and how it teaches us to avoid experimentation and the necessary failure associated with it. My favourite quote from his talk is the following:

If you're not prepared to be wrong then you will never come up with anything original.

And in an ever-changing, complex world, we are increasingly being tasked with developing original ideas, products and services. In order to solve these new problems, we will undoubtedly have some failures along the way.

Technological entrepreneurship is a great microcosm in which to view failure. Most people have heard of college dropouts Bill Gates (co-founder of Microsoft) and Steve Jobs (co-founder of Apple); who went on the become some of the wealthiest and most influential people in the world. What fewer people know is they both had some spectacular failures during their careers. Jobs got kicked out of Apple and then started the commercially unsuccessful NeXT. Gates' first company Traf-O-Data was anything but successful and under his watch Microsoft produced some amazing failures including Windows ME, Microsoft Bob and the music player Zune. But history tells us that within these failures were the seeds of success. The lessons learnt from their earlier failures helped propel both men towards huge success. They needed to fail before they could be successful.

We touched on this earlier, but it warrants repeating again. Customers often don't know upfront what they want and although they may give us some initial requirements, success often relies on IKIWISI. Often we have to build for them what they say they want, so that can recognize that it is not what they want, and this takes us one step closer to success. Building the wrong thing is often an important and necessary step toward building the right thing.

Only results

Although it may appear contradictory, from another viewpoint the Agile Mindset doesn't recognise failure at all; it only recognises results. We do some work, get some results and then we check those results. When we take a scientific approach and look upon all our work as experiments, then it follows that all we will get is results.

Bab Shiv, Professor of Marketing at Stanford Graduate School of Business, whose research focuses on innovation in the workplace cites Google as an example of a company which has embraced the "only results" experimental mindset.

One thing all companies can and should do is encourage a culture of innovation at all levels, the way Google has. "Small teams within Google run 3,000 to 5,000 experiments a year," says Shiv. "A manager there might say, 'We should use this course of action,' and a new hire might say, 'I think this way of doing it will be better.' That manager's first reaction isn't resistance, it's 'OK, let's test it.' That's the great thing about Google. There are no egos when it comes to opinions," he says. "There's data." (28)

Failure-friendly mindset

The Agile Mindset can be considered failure-friendly. It takes the position, backed up by Carol Dweck's research into fixed and growth mindsets, that how you approach failure can actually determine your path to success.

In a fixed mindset, you believe your abilities are relatively defined and static — which means that every task becomes a test to prove yourself. This leads you to overemphasize outcomes and the trappings of success, react with defensiveness toward setbacks, and hang back from opportunities. Everything is win or lose, seen more as a zero-sum game.

In contrast, the growth mindset is based on the belief that your skills can improve, develop, and grow. You approach challenges, setbacks, and achievements with a sense of possibility, which affects how you view your history and then pave the way forward. As Dweck writes: "[M]indsets change what people strive for and what they see as success. How they change the definition, significance, and impact of failure. And they change the deepest meaning of effort." (29)

Psychological Safety

> You don't make mistakes, mistakes make you.
>
> -Avani Patel, Head of Harvard Business School StartUp Studio

By pretty much any way you measure it, Google is a very successful organization. Never one to rest on their laurels, they undertook a two-year study to discover the factors which contributed to high performing teams. Psychological Safety made the top of their list.

Psychological safety was far and away the most important of the five dynamics we found -- it's the underpinning of the other four. How could that be? Taking a risk around your team members seems simple. But remember the last time you were working on a project. Did you feel like you could ask what the goal was without the risk of sounding like you're the only one out of the loop? Or did you opt for continuing without clarifying anything, in order to avoid being perceived as someone who is unaware?

Turns out, we're all reluctant to engage in behaviors that could negatively influence how others perceive our competence, awareness, and positivity. Although this kind of self-protection is a natural strategy in the workplace, it is detrimental to effective teamwork. On the flip side, the safer team members feel with one another, the more likely they are to admit mistakes, to partner, and to take on new roles. And it affects pretty much every important dimension we look at for employees. Individuals on teams with higher psychological safety are less likely to leave Google, they're more likely to harness the power of diverse ideas from their teammates, they bring in more revenue, and they're rated as effective twice as often by executives. (30)

Psychological safety isn't about being nice. It's about giving candid feedback, openly admitting mistakes, and learning from each other. And one of the most straight-forward ways of moving towards Psychological Safety is to reframe work in your organisation as a leaning problem, rather than an execution problem, and embrace a culture of continuous learning and improvement as we discussed earlier (31).

Psychological safety, as we shall see in this section, is very closely aligned with trust and the feeling amongst team members that it is safe to fail.

Safe to fail

We saw earlier with the Cynefin framework that the best way to deal with complex problems is using a process of probe-sense-respond. These probes are also called experiments, spikes, sprints or iterations. The key is that these probes need to be safe-to-fail. If we are acting under great uncertainty and interacting with a complex system, then there can be no guarantee of success.

Writing on the Cognitive Edge blog, Cynefin creator David Snowden writes:

Safe-fail Probes are small-scale experiments that approach issues from different angles, in small and safe-to-fail ways, the intent of which is to approach issues in small, contained ways to allow emergent possibilities to become more visible. The emphasis, then, is not on ensuring success or avoiding failure, but in allowing ideas that are not useful to fail in small, contained and tolerable ways. The ideas that do produce observable benefits can then be adopted and amplified when the complex system has shown the appropriate response to its stimulus. Where systems and the environments in which they exist become increasingly complex, what is known and what can be planned for becomes less certain – introducing and increasing organisational tolerance for failure is more crucial than ever. (32)

So if psychological safety is so important, how do we go about increasing the safety in teams and organisations? We start with transparency and trust.

Transparency and Trust

Trust is defined as a belief in the reliability, truth, or ability of someone or something. Much has been written about trust and Agile but possibly the most pertinent is that Trust is The Unspoken Element of Being Agile. (33).

Trust is also a highly emotive word and one that some people may be uncomfortable with discussing in relation to their work. After all, many people just want to get on with their jobs without all this "touchy-feely" stuff.

What first came to your mind when you thought about trust? The chances are that it may not have been the members of your current team. But as Paul Santagata, Head of Industry at Google says "There's no team without trust". Trust is so important that it may be the most important factor that differentiates highly successful Agile teams from the ordinary.

Trust is at the core of any functioning agile team. Trust is the foundation needed for any team to function. In his book, Five Dysfunctions of a Team, Patrick Lencioni creates a model in which trust is the basis for all other constructive team behaviours. Without trust we cannot build creative conflict, be committed, exercise accountability, and strive for common goals. (34)

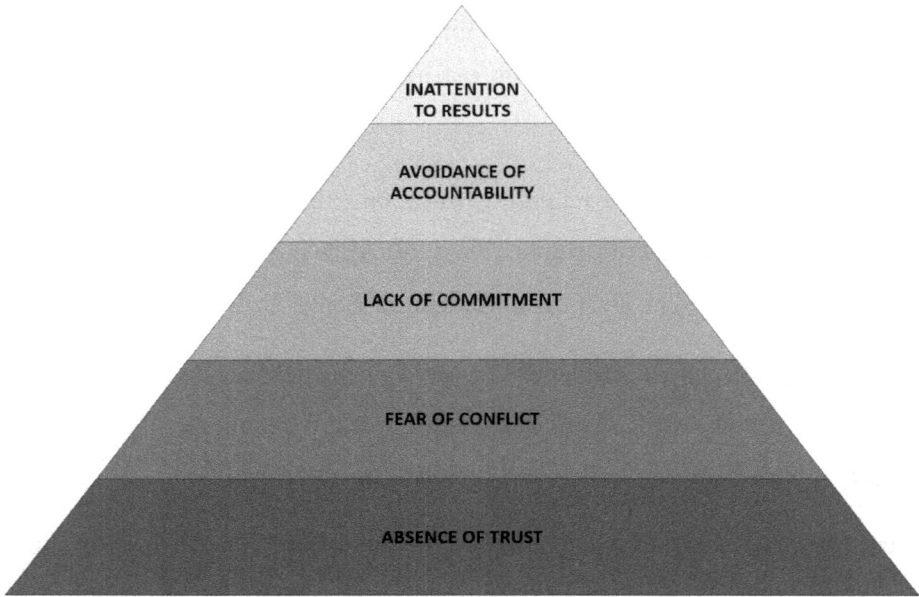

Figure 16. The Five Dysfunctions of a Team

Trust is so fundamental to creating a fail-safe environment that a formula has been devised to measure the level of trust within teams.

The Trust formula

A formula for trust has been developed by the team at Trusted Advisor.

$$T = C + R + I / S$$

Trustworthiness = Credibility + Reliability + Intimacy all divided by Self-orientation.

Trustworthiness is the Trust Quotient (TQ). The Trust Quotient is a number — like your IQ or EQ — that benchmarks your trustworthiness against the four variables.

Let's dig into each variable a bit more:

Credibility has to do with the words we speak. In a sentence we might say, "I can trust what she says about intellectual property; she's very credible on the subject."

Reliability has to do with actions. We might say, "If he says he'll deliver the product tomorrow, I trust him, because he's dependable."

Intimacy refers to the safety or security that we feel when entrusting someone with something. We might say, "I can trust her with that information; she's never violated my confidentiality before, and she would never embarrass me."

Self-orientation refers to a person's focus. In particular, whether the person's focus is primarily on him or herself, or on the other person. We might say, "I can't trust him on this deal — I don't think he cares enough about me, he's focused on what he gets out of it." Or more commonly, "I don't trust him — I think he's too concerned about how he's appearing, so he's not really paying attention." (35)

Trust is used in Agile in place of control. We give our teams a broad set of guidelines or goals and then let them self-organise about how they achieve these results.

If trust boils down to one thing then it is likely to be vulnerability. In his book "Overcoming The Five Dysfunctions Of A Team" Patrick Lencioni explains that trust is all about vulnerability, 'Team members need to be comfortable being exposed to one another, so that they will be unafraid to honestly say things like "I was wrong," "I made a mistake," "I need help," "I'm not sure," "you're better than I am at that," and "I'm sorry."' (36)

Trust goes hand-in-hand with transparency. If we are going to make ourselves vulnerable and make our work transparent, for example showing our work progress on a public Kanban board for all to see, then we cannot also have management scrutinize and micro-manage that which we have made public. The two behaviours cannot co-exist in the long-term. The key driver for transparency is the benefit that the whole team gets from having full visibility of their own work. When a team makes their work transparent, they also must be trusted by management to complete that work on their own terms.

Now that we have established the importance of trust, let's look at some ways of building trust.

Zak's strategies to create trust

Similar to Lencioni, the Agile Mindset sees trust as the fundamental building block on which high performing teams are built. While it does take time and perseverance to build trust, there are definite strategies that we can implement to get results.

Paul J. Zak, Harvard researcher and author of "The Trust Factor: The Science of Creating High Performing Companies," has invested decades researching the neurological connection between trust, leadership, and organizational performance. Over his two decades of research, Zak discovered that "compared with people at low-trust companies, people at high-trust companies report 74% less stress, 106% more energy at work, 50% higher productivity, 13% fewer sick days, 76% more engagement, 29% more satisfaction with their lives, and 40% less burnout." (37)

Through his experiments and surveys, Zak identified eight management behaviours that foster trust in teams and organisations.

1. Recognize excellence

2. Induce "challenge stress."

3. Give people discretion in how they do their work.

4. Enable job crafting

5. Share information broadly

6. Intentionally build relationships

7. Facilitate whole-person growth

8. Show vulnerability (38)

We have explored trust and found that it is one of the cornerstones underpinning the Agile Mindset, and we have looked at ways of measuring and increasing the levels of trust within teams. Once we have established a high level of trust, we can do something which may sound a little unusual at first, but is very cool; Celebrate Failure.

Celebrate Failure

Spotify is a Swedish entertainment company specializing in media streaming and well-known for their internal Agile model involving Squads, Chapters, Tribes and Guilds. What is less well known is their revolutionary approach to failure.

Spotify is the epitome of a fail-friendly culture. To the point where some of the squads at Spotify have their own failure walls, where they can publically share their failures and the lessons learnt from them. This serves a double purpose. On the one hand, this works to normalize mistakes and failures, and on the other hand it allows all the other teams to benefit from the lessons learned. At Spotify they focus on Failure Recovery rather than Failure Avoidance and sometimes they even celebrate failure with cake! (39) Other organisations have taken to promoting the *failure bow* as a way of removing the shame and pain of failure and turning it into an experience that leads to better results (40).

But Spotify are far from the only successful organization that celebrates failure. India's Tata group awards an annual prize for the best failed idea. Intuit, the software company, and Eli Lilly, the pharmaceuticals firm, have both taken to holding failure parties. P&G encourages employees to talk about their failures as well as their successes during performance reviews. Leaders should remember how often failure paves the way for success. Henry Ford got nowhere with his first two attempts to start a car company. But that did not stop him. (41)

Within the Agile Mindset, failure is normalized and expected. As mentioned earlier, we do not aim to fail but recognize and accept that it will happen.

When the players expect to be wrong sometimes – and not due to incompetence – an interesting shift takes place. (42)

With this in mind, we embrace failure and use it to our advantage through an approach called *Fail Fast*.

Fail Fast

Fall seven times. Stand up eight.

-Old Japanese Proverb

Once we have established an environment where it is safe to fail, we then want to fail as fast as possible.

Spotify founder Daniel Ek describes one of their key business strategies as "We aim to make mistakes faster than anyone else". The idea behind it is that along the product development cycle we're going to make mistakes and this is inevitable. So, why not fail fast when we do fail? Each failure is also an opportunity to learn! It's a strategy for long-term success.

Failure can take many forms. It could be a feature, it could be product-market fit, it could be the business model, the choice of a cofounder, a hire, or the whole idea of starting a business in the first place. Fail fast does not apply to all of these categories. If you do a lot of market research, are passionate about an idea, start a business with your best friend, work at it for a time, but struggle to get the business off the ground, does that mean you should fail fast and shut the business down? Of course not. Fail fast isn't about the big issues, it's about the little ones. It's an approach to running a company or developing a product that embraces lots of little experiments with the idea that some will work and grow and others will fail and die. (43)

International design and consulting firm IDEO combines structured brainstorming, rapid prototyping and field research to rapidly try out new concepts and get to good products. They know that any one single idea is likely bad — for instance, only 12 in 4,000 are actually successful. But the idea is to embrace the rapid production of those bad ideas to get to the good ones. (44)

Small bets

"If you're trying to solve a problem there are potentially hundreds of possible pathways to take, but only a few are going to lead to the appropriate solution. And the only way to discover that is to try and fail and try again," says Baba Shiv, a professor at Stanford Graduate School of Business whose research focuses on innovation in the workplace. (28)

The idea of placing small bets is similar to the scientific mindset in acknowledging that the outcome of our actions may be negative, however the terms *bet* clearly indicates that we are taking a risk that could have zero return.

In his book *Little Bets*, Peter Sims explains how placing small bets is the winning strategy shared commonly amongst a broad range of successful people including Apple CEO Steve Jobs, comedian Chris Rock, inventor Thomas Edison, prize-winning architect Frank Gehry, and the story developers at Pixar films.

Little bets are a way to explore and develop new possibilities. Specifically, a little bet is a low-risk action taken to discover, develop, and test an idea. Chris Rock develops new comedy routines by making little bets with small audiences; Amazon's CEO Jeff Bezos makes small bets to identify opportunities in new markets like cloud computing. Little bets are at the centre of an approach to get to the right idea without getting stymied by perfectionism, risk-aversion, or excessive planning.

How is this approach different from and better than the typical way most people do something new?

We're taught from an early age to use certain procedures and rules to analyse and solve problems, such as for math or chemistry. There's an emphasis on minimizing errors and avoiding failure. These skills serve us extremely well when we have enough information to put into a formula or plan. But what happens when we don't even know what problems we're trying to solve? In those kinds of situations, engaging in a process of discovery and making little bets complements more linear, procedural thinking. (45)

Feedback loops

The reason we want to fail fast is so that we can learn fast. This is why many Agile teams employ several types of feedback loops; daily stand-ups, weekly or bi-weekly reviews, and retrospectives. These enable fast feedback to be received, processed and acted upon.

For comparison, consider the slow feedback loop example of the "lessons learned" sessions traditionally conducted at the end of traditional projects. While these sessions are undoubtedly of some value, unfortunately to a large degree they are akin to shutting the gate after the horse has bolted. Once the project has finished, it is too late for the lessons to have any benefit to the project they came from. But when we have rapid feedback loops, we are able to benefit from the learnings and incorporate these benefits into the same project that they came from, and much earlier in the process than had we waited until the end of the project.

Think about dynamic speed displays: a speed limit posting coupled with a radar sensor attached to a huge digital readout announcing "Your Speed." These provide almost real-time feedback to the driver and give them the opportunity to learn from the feedback and adjust their speed if necessary. What is so good about this? After all we could just record any speeding vehicles details and then issue them with a fine afterwards (this is akin to the post-project lessons learned session). Consider though that our goal is to actually get the cars to lower their speed, and through fast feedback we are able to achieve this goal. In Agile the same applies. We are generally trying to deliver maximum value and fast feedback gets us closer to delivering that that value, in less time. (46)

Pivots

Let us assume that we have placed our small bet and received fast feedback. Unfortunately, our small bet or experiment has failed. What are we to do next?

The answer is that next we must Pivot. Originating in the Lean Startup movement, a pivot is a structured course correction designed to test a new fundamental hypothesis about the product, strategy, and engine of growth. (47). Steve Blank, adjunct professor of entrepreneurship at Stanford, puts it another way; it's about firing the plan rather than the executive. (48)

Pivots come in many different flavours, each designed to test the viability of a different hypothesis about the product, business model, and engine of growth. There are 10 types of pivot defined by Eric Ries.

1. Zoom-in pivot. In this case, what previously was considered a single feature in a product becomes the whole product. This highlights the value of "focus" and "minimum viable product" (MVP), delivered quickly and efficiently.

2. Zoom-out pivot. In the reverse situation, sometimes a single feature is insufficient to support a customer set. In this type of pivot, what was considered the whole product becomes a single feature of a much larger product.

3. Customer segment pivot. Your product may attract real customers, but not the ones in the original vision. In other words, it solves a real problem, but needs to be positioned for a more appreciative segment, and optimised for that segment.

4. Customer need pivot. Early customer feedback indicates that the problem solved is not very important, or money isn't available to buy. This requires repositioning, or a completely new product, to find a problem worth solving.

5. Platform pivot. This refers to a change from an application to a platform, or vice versa. Many founders envision their solution as a platform for future products, but don't have a single killer application just yet. Most customers buy solutions, not platforms.

6. Business architecture pivot. Geoffrey Moore, many years ago, observed that there are two major business architectures: high margin, low volume (complex systems model), or low margin, high volume (volume operations model). You can't do both at the same time.

7. Value capture pivot. This refers to the monetization or revenue model. Changes to the way a startup captures value can have far-reaching consequences for business, product, and marketing strategies. The "free" model doesn't capture much value.

8. Engine of growth pivot. Most startups these days use one of three primary growth engines: the viral, sticky, and paid growth models. Picking the right model can dramatically affect the speed and profitability of growth.

9. Channel pivot. In sales terminology, the mechanism by which a company delivers it product to customers is called the sales channel or distribution channel. Channel pivots usually require unique pricing, feature, and competitive positioning adjustments.

10. Technology pivot. Sometimes a startup discovers a way to achieve the same solution by using a completely different technology. This is most relevant if the new technology can provide superior price and performance to improve competitive posture. (49)

How powerful are pivots? Some of the most successful companies started life with very different goals and made one or more significant pivots before evolving into the companies that they are today. Here are some pertinent examples.

- Before getting into video games, Nintendo has produced everything from playing cards to vacuum cleaners, and instant rice

- Coupon site Groupon started life as The Point, a website where users could start a campaign asking people to give money or do something as a group - but only once a 'tipping point' of people agree to participate.

- Phone manufacturer Nokia began life as a paper mill in 1865 before moving into rubber manufacturing and finally into phones.

- Photo sharing app Instagram started out as a location-based service called Burbn.

- Wrigley founder William Wrigley was a salesman of items such as soap and baking powder, who used to give chewing gum away.

- YouTube was originally a video dating site.

- Facebook started out as Facemash, a site which showed two pictures of people next to each other and asking the user to identify which one was 'hotter.'

- Starbucks was originally a supplier of coffee beans and espresso makers.

- Automotive company Suzuki a purveyor of weaving loom machines famous for powering the Japanese silk industry.

We can see from these examples that pivots can be extremely powerful. What all these companies have in common is that they didn't view failure as an end-point, but rather as a learning experience and an opportunity to try something new.

Summary

Failure is a highly emotional word and something that we are generally educated throughout our lives to avoid and to cover up. The Agile Mindset takes a very different view of failure. Obviously, we don't want to fail, but if we are constantly trying new things within an uncertain and changing environment, then some failures are almost certain to occur. We approach failure by anticipating it and by failing-fast through executing lots of small safe-to-fail bets. We examine the results of each bet and then pivot towards making a new safe-to-fail bet. When failures occur, we celebrate them, learn what we can from them, and then share these learning widely amongst our organisation. High levels of trust and psychological safety are absolutely essential to be able to operate with these levels of transparency and openness.

Key Points

- Most of us have been educated to fear failure.
- In uncertain and changing environments, some failures are almost certain to occur.
- Celebrate failures so as to normalise their occurrence.
- Failure is often a necessary precursor to success.
- Psychological safety is critical for developing a failure-friendly environment.
- High levels of trust are crucial for operating with high levels of trust and transparency.
- Fail fast by placing many small safe-to-fail bets.
- Pivots are a powerful way of changing direction after a failure.

Grab your free Agile mindset resources at

www.SchoolOfInnovation.net.

Key #4. Learning

The only sustainable competitive advantage is an organization's ability to learn faster than the competition.

-Peter Senge, Author of *The Fifth Discipline*

In the previous chapter, we looked at failure in some depth. The point of failure, if you like, is to learn from it. Learning is what gives value to failure. Some people even take the view that we should deliberately fail so that we can create learning. But learning isn't always appreciated in organisations and teams. In some respects, there is an assumption that we should already have learnt all that we need to know and just get on with using what we already know. But in an uncertain changing world, success often goes to those who learn the fastest.

In this chapter, we will look at how learning is an integral part of the Agile Mindset and how it ties in with the concepts of Uncertainty, Change and Failure that we have explored so far.

In my parent's generation, people went to high school and then maybe on to an apprenticeship, college or university. But after that point, unless you were an academic, learning effectively stopped. This has been called the "inoculation" theory of education — "I got my degree (or diploma), and now I don't have to learn any more". (50). You went to work for the next 40 years and used the skills you had learnt. Conditions hardly changed, and if they did change, then they changed quite slowly.

The truth is that learning didn't actually stop but people never talked about it or focused on learning as they do now. Lifelong learning was not a concept that people talked about back then. But nowadays learning can reach its expiry date rather quickly. Professional services firm EY interviewed more than 3000 students, employers, university leaders, policymakers and observers. They concluded that within a decade 40% of all existing university degrees could be obsolete. (51)

In contrast to the traditional mindset that learning finishes once we enter the workforce, the Agile Mindset sees learning as a constant and never-ending process in response to an ever-changing world. In fact learning is seen as so important at Google that they have made it their number one hiring criteria:

For every job, though, the No. 1 thing we look for is general cognitive ability, and it's not I.Q. It's learning ability. It's the ability to process on the fly. It's the ability to pull together disparate bits of information. We assess that using structured behavioral interviews that we validate to make sure they're predictive. (52)

Continuous learning

The illiterate of the 21st century will not be those who cannot read and write, but those who cannot learn, unlearn, and relearn.

-Alvin Toffler

Continuous improvement, lifelong learning and the learning organization are all terms that have entered the general lexicon. In this section, we will look at how the Agile Mindset embraces, and is substantially built upon, the idea of continuous learning at both a macro and micro level.

The Learning organization

In 1990, American systems scientist Peter Senge's book *The Fifth Discipline* introduced the world to the concept of the learning organisation. Senge was a pioneer in recognising that in an ever-changing, uncertain and globally connected world, the only sustainable competitive advantage is to be able to learn faster than your competitors; everything else can and will be copied.

Learning as a competitive advantage was a very novel idea when first introduced but it still remains extremely powerful today. While many leaders will pay lip service to the idea of continuous learning, it appears that the true hidden power of the concept still eludes many.

There are five key ideas which flow from adopting this aspect of the Agile Mindset.

Firstly, as we discussed earlier, there is a quite significant mindset shift that acknowledges that learning continues to take place in the workforce and does not stop one university or trade school is completed.

Secondly, it acknowledges that the environment is constantly changing. If this was not true, and the environment was static, then we wouldn't need to continue learning because conceivably at some point we would reach a complete understanding and not need to learn anymore.

Thirdly, it acknowledges that we do not have, and can never have all the answers upfront. So we must begin without complete knowledge upfront and continue to operate with incomplete knowledge.

Fourthly, learning implies failure. Very few people get 100% on a test the first time they take it. So some failure should be expected.

Lastly, it highlights the need to capture and share knowledge within teams and amongst the larger organisation.

There are a number of different techniques for implementing continuous learning. Some of the most popular include:

- Communities of practice (Spotify guilds)

- Wikis

- Retrospectives

- Stand-ups

- Information radiators

- Pair programming (for software development)

- Code reviews (for software development)

Kaizen

Forty years earlier, on the other side of the Pacific Ocean from Senge, Toyota in Japan implemented quality circles which lead to the development of the Toyota Production System and Kaizen, the practice of continually learning and continually making improvements.

We discussed Kaizen earlier, but it is such a crucial part of the Lean philosophy that we will explore it further, this time with a focus on the continuous learning aspect.

Kaizen is based on ten principles as listed below:

1. Improve everything continuously.

2. Abolish old, traditional concepts.

3. Accept no excuses and make things happen.

4. Say no to the status quo of implementing new methods and assuming they will work.

5. If something is wrong, correct it.

6. Empower everyone to take part in problem solving.

7. Get information and opinions from multiple people.

8. Before making decisions, ask "why" five times to get to the root cause. (5 Why Method)

9. Be economical. Save money through small improvements and spend the saved money on further improvements.

10. Remember that improvement has no limits. Never stop trying to improve. (53)

Note how most of the Kaizen principles relate to continuous learning and continuous improvement.

Kaizen and Lean offer a fundamentally different approach to problem-solving than most traditional companies practice. It's a "learn-by-doing" method that involves the people doing the work in improving the work right now. Most companies delegate important problems to teams of experts that take months to create a plan and even longer to get lasting improvements.

Adopting lean through a kaizen "learn-by-doing" approach is radically different—a "doing" activity as opposed to the "planning" activity described above. (54)

One of the often overlooked, but potentially most valuable, aspects of Kaizen is that it gives us permission to start where we are and make continual improvements as we progress. We don't have to wait until we are perfect before making a start.

Lifelong learning

One of the most well-known quotes from author and motivational speaker Zig Ziglar is the following:

The only thing worse than training an employee and having them leave, is to not train them, and have them stay.

And in an ever-changing uncertain world, not training your people, not having them continually learning, appears to be a recipe for disaster for many organisations.

However, it appears that not everyone got the memo, as research indicates that on-the-job training is on the decline. In its 2015 Economic Report of the President, America's Council of Economic Advisers found that the share of the country's workers receiving either paid-for or on-the-job training had fallen steadily between 1996 and 2008. In Britain the average amount of training received by workers almost halved between 1997 and 2009, to just 0.69 hours a week. (55)

Rather than take this data to mean that continuous learning isn't necessary, it is more useful to consider that not every company will employ a lifelong learning strategy at either an organisational nor individual level. But neither will every organization survive. Just look at one-time seemingly indestructible mainstays such as Kodak, Pan Am and Thomas Cook. Could there be a connection between organizational failure and ignorance of the importance of having a culture of continual learning? I suspect that it is at least a contributing factor. As Scott Atkinson put it in the Harvard Business Review:

Kodak remains a sad story of potential lost. The American icon had the talent, the money, and even the foresight to make the transition. Instead it ended up the victim of the aftershocks of a disruptive change. Learn the right lessons, and you can avoid its fate. (56)

The alternative is to adopt the Agile Mindset and embrace continuous learning.

Continuous learning is a "learning culture", a community of workers continuously and collectively seeking performance improvement through new knowledge, new skills, and new applications of knowledge and skills to achieve the goals of the organization. A learning culture is a culture of inquiry; an environment in which employees feel safe asking tough questions about the purpose and quality of what they are doing for customers, themselves, and other stakeholders. (57)

Create knowledge

An investment in knowledge pays the best interest.

–Benjamin Franklin

"There is no fool like an old fool" says the popular international proverb. One of the meanings of this proverb is that people can make mistakes but they should learn from them. You are not a fool if you make a mistake but you become one if you make the same mistake again. It simply means that you're not learning. (58)

So what is the point of all this learning? The point is to create knowledge, or to be more precise to create *new* knowledge. This is different from knowledge management, which is concerned with managing the knowledge that we already have.

Knowledge is different from information or data. Knowledge resides in individuals. For information and data to turn into knowledge it must firstly be readily available, and secondly it must be acted upon – it must have some effect on how we do things.

Creating knowledge is an integral part of the Agile process.

We build in stages so as to discover what the customer needs and then build it. By doing it this way we deliver value quickly and avoid building things of lesser (or no) value. We believe that software development is more a discovery process than a building process. (59)

Harley Davidson, for example, placed a very high priority on creating knowledge through their set-based product development process, described as follows:

set-based development is a carefully orchestrated development process that exploits the learning principles of experimental learning cycles to explore the limits of a design to understand the risks. (60)

Create Knowledge is also one of the core principles of Lean Software Development.

Planning is useful, but learning is essential. You want to promote strategies, such as iterative development, that help teams discover what stakeholders really want and act on that knowledge. It's also important for a team to regularly reflect on what they're doing and then act to improve their approach. (61)

Let's be clear, creating knowledge this does not mean creating excessive amounts of documentation. It actually means creating knowledge. As Albert Einstein famously said:

Knowledge is experience, everything else is just information.

Every time we conduct an experiment and it fails, we gather new knowledge that we can use in the future.

Your team should not only learn and teach each other - they should be able to solve all kinds of problems in a structured way e.g. Plan Do Check Act (PDCA). The team should often behave like small research institute, they should establish hypotheses and conduct many rapid experiments in order to verify them. Your team should also produce concise and valuable documentation keeping up to date knowledge base of what works and what doesn't, and then implement the best alternative. (58)

Multiple levels of learning

> Learn continually - there's always "one more thing" to learn!
>
> -Steve Jobs

We have seen that the Agile Mindset is one that is continually learning as we experiment in a complex and uncertain changing environment. While Agile teams and organisations learn about many things over time, most of the knowledge created is concentrated in three main areas; Product, People and Process. In this section we will look at how learning takes place in each of these areas in more detail.

Learning about Product

At the beginning of a project, the product we want to build only exists as an idea. We generally then expand this idea into a set of requirements; a more detailed description of what we want to build. As we move through the process of building our product, our product conceptually exists in two parts; the part that we have actually built, and the part that we have yet to build (the requirements). So the requirements and the finished product are interlinked and in some ways they are part of the same whole.

In predictive methodologies there was an assumption that we could capture all of the product requirements upfront before any building had commenced. And not just capture the requirements but capture them to a very detailed level. You might recognize this as being based on the rationalists *A priori* view that we discussed earlier, the idea that knowledge is knowable in advance.

As we learned earlier, the Agile Mindset is based on empiricism, which is often implemented through a Plan-Do-Check-Act cycle or a similar mechanism. Where Agile really differs from predictive methods is through a process called Progress Elaboration.

Progress Elaboration

In predictive project approaches it is common to engage in Big Design Up Front (DBUF), which involves defining all of the project requirements, upfront, down to a very granular level. BDUF as the name suggests, occurs at the beginning of the project before any building or development work commences.

By now you might be able to see some of the weaknesses in this approach. Defining all requirements to a granular level can be an exhaustive process and one that does not readily embrace subsequent change to those requirements. As well as leaving no room for change, it also leaves no room for learning. And if we do learn new knowledge or need to change or adapt, it means that we may have wasted a large amount of effort in designs that are no longer relevant.

In Agile we don't practice BDUF. Instead we practice Progressive Elaboration.

In the Traditional sense, Progressive Elaboration involves an iterative process of increasing the level of detail in a project management plan as greater amounts of information and more accurate estimates become available throughout the project life cycle. Progressive Elaboration for Agile project teams is a bit different because activities are not extensively planned at the project outset. Requirements are progressively elaborated from the 'Mile-High' Level to the '1-Foot' Level at varying times throughout the project and the Agile development team focuses specifically on known project aspects. (62)

In Agile we are continually learning about the product that we are building. We expect requirements to change as we validate what we have built and determine if our hypotheses actually meet the customers' needs.

For any product we are building, and especially true for knowledge-based or technology products, the chances are that we haven't built this product before. If we haven't done something before then we need to learn how to do it, we can't just be expected to know upfront. And when it comes to our product then we need to learn about how to build *this* product; how the pieces fit together and interact with each other. For problems of a Complex nature we cannot know how the component pieces will interact with each ahead of time. We need to Sense, Probe and Respond which is another way of saying that we need to continually learn about the product we are building.

Learning about People

In any work effort there are various groups of people involved. At a minimum we will typically have our internal team members, stakeholders (with a vested interest in the work) and other people within our organization, external partners, and customers.

Most of us will have interacted with these groups throughout our careers, however we may not have worked with this exact group people beforehand i.e. we may have dealt with stakeholders but not these particular stakeholders. The same applies to all the other groups identified earlier. And as with most things Agile, we want to continually improve – to get better at how we interact and work with each group of people.

It is increasingly common for teams to form around a piece of work, complete the work and then disband as the team members go off individually and join other teams to work on other projects. Interestingly, this is the model that the film industry has worked on for decades, where most people operate as independent entities who come together to work on a film (the piece of work) and then disband after the film is complete.

Even if we have worked with the same people beforehand, we may not have worked in this specific Agile way with them, or we may not have worked on this type of problem with them. Because each situation is different we will have to learn, to some degree, how to work together on each project we work on.

All new teams need to *learn* how to work together. Often this will require the team to progress through Tuckman's four stages of team development(Figure 18); Storming, Norming, Forming and Performing; until the team reaches a state of high performance.

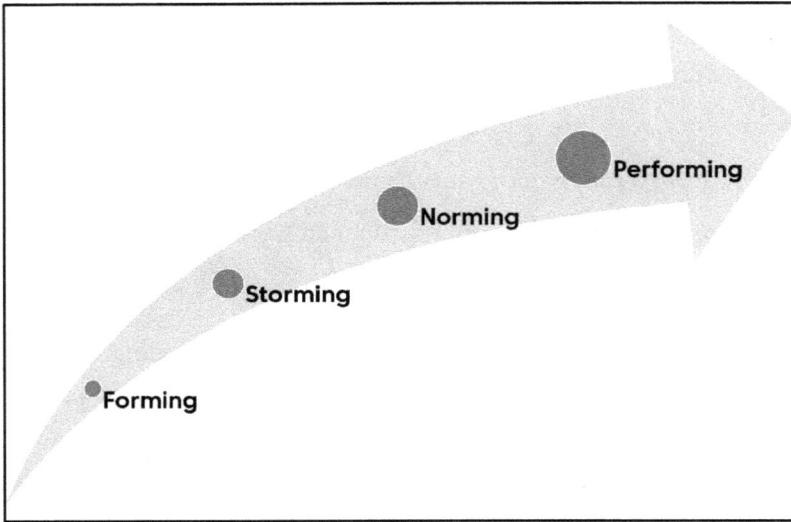

Figure 17. Tuckman's model of group development

Similarly, the team will need to learn how to work effectively with new stakeholders. There may be familiarity with the rest of the organization but the dynamics may be changing, for example there is a big difference on working on some small background project, compared to a mission-critical project that the company has bet its future on.

External partners can be challenging to work with at the best of times, and the chances are that even if you have engaged with the external partner before, you are likely to have to deal with different individuals over time.

Te customers base is forever changing in composition and in terms of wants and needs. Even if the customer base was relatively stable we might be interacting with them in a different way; for example, we may have produced a customer website but building a mobile app for the same group is still a different proposition.

Learning about Process

People build the product through a process. And just as we need to continually learn about the people and the product we are building, we also need to learn about the process we use to build our product.

Most traditional project models, plans, and tools make a critical assumption about the goal of a Produce Development (PD) project that is quite limiting in practice, even when the goal is known and fixed. These models assume that the path to reach the goal (i.e., a predetermined set of activities and dependencies) is known and will be sufficiently efficient and effective. Yet, this is rarely the reality in PD: the planned set of activities may be both insufficient and partly unnecessary. When the path to the destination is unclear, it is no wonder that so many PD projects are "challenged" or fail. For example, in a survey of over 250 000 small software PD projects, the Standish Group reports that only 28% succeeded, while 23% failed and 49% were "challenged," meaning they were either late, over budget, or had fewer features or functions than originally specified. (63)

Without a culture of learning, processes take over that allow us to wriggle out of responsibility — a mindset encapsulated in the phrase: "I didn't fail. The Agile methods don't work." (38)

At its core, Agile is adaptive. Many people only see adaptivity in the context of a project frequently adapting to meet the changing requirements of its customers. However, there's another angle to adaptivity: that of the process changing over time. A project that begins using an adaptive process won't have the same process a year later. Over time, the team will find what works for them, and alter the process to fit. (64)

Summary

Learning was once upon a time seen as something that only really took place in an educational setting. As the world has become more complex and rapidly changing, many have taken the view that learning is a continuous and ongoing process. This is the view of the Agile Mindset and it sees this learning taking place continuously across the board; at the macro level and at the micro-level.

The learning process should create knowledge; information that is readily available and acted upon. Agile teams often create and incorporate this knowledge through periodic inspection and adaption at meetings such as Retrospectives. Knowledge should also be shared quickly and widely amongst the team and the wider organization to obtain the greatest benefit.

Learning occurs on multiple levels. We continue to learn about the Product we are building, the People involved, and the Process of the building the product. Holding the mindset and expectation of continual learning allows us to gain all of the continuous improvement benefits of Kaizen which served Japanese industry so well.

Key Points

- When dealing with complex, uncertain and changing environments we cannot reasonably be expected to know everything upfront. There are many things that we will need to learn along the way.

- Learning takes place throughout our lifetime, not just in an education setting.

- Learning should create knowledge; information that is accessible and actioned.

- The Kaizen philosophy of continual improvement is also one of continuous learning.

- On any project we should continually learn about Product, People and Process.

Remember to get this book's supplementary resources from www.SchoolOfInnovation.net.

Key #5. People

Consider two scenarios. In scenario A, you have the best processes and tools imaginable in the hands of average people. In scenario B, you have average tools and processes in the hands of the best people imaginable. Which scenario would you prefer?

Your answer may reveal a lot about how you view people. If you chose scenario A then you may have been heavily influenced by the scientific management ideas of Frederick Taylor (Figure 19), also known as Taylorism, which permeated much of management thinking during the 20th century. And who could blame you? Most organisations nowadays have a Human Resources (HR) function. That word, *Resources*, groups humans alongside other categories of resources such as finance, raw materials and plant and equipment.

Figure 18. Frederick Winslow Taylor

Perhaps such a term made sense in the industrialised 19th century where thousands of largely uneducated people started working in repetitive factory jobs.

Henry Ford and Alfred Sloan created the 'big company' as we know it, and revolutionized how companies worked. Today, it's more like 'I want a girlfriend, I create Facebook'.

– Richard Donkin, The Future of Work

But the Agile Mindset concurs that the 21st-century knowledge worker needs to be treated very differently. They need to be recognised as people, as human beings motivated by purpose, mastery and autonomy rather than fear and control (65).

In this chapter we will look at some of the key theories of human motivation and behaviour and how they are represented in the Agile Mindset.

Theory Y

With every passing year, McGregor's message becomes ever more relevant, more timely, and more important.

-Peter F. Drucker, *Douglas McGregor, Revisited: Managing the Human Side of Enterprise*

Theory X and Theory Y are theories of human motivation and management. They were created and developed during the 1960s by Douglas McGregor, a founding faculty member of MIT's Sloan School of Management, and first appeared in his book *The Human Side of Enterprise*.

These two theories describe contrasting models of workforce motivation, each with opposing sets of general assumptions of how workers are motivated. These assumptions form the basis for two different managerial styles.

Theory X concurs with the Taylorist viewpoint, and stresses the importance of strict supervision, external rewards, and penalties, In contrast, Theory Y highlights the motivating role of job satisfaction and encourages workers to approach tasks without direct supervision.

In this section we will delve more deeply into Theory X and Theory Y, contrast the two theories and look at how these theories relate to the Agile Mindset. I will also let you in on what I call the "secret sauce", the part of McGregor's theory which many people do not understand and which prevents many individuals and organisations from getting the highest value out of McGregor's work.

The Theories

The Economist magazine describes the theories as follows.

Theory X is an authoritarian style where the emphasis is on "productivity, on the concept of a fair day's work, on the evils of feather-bedding and restriction of output, on rewards for performance ... [it] reflects an underlying belief that management must counteract an inherent human tendency to avoid work". Theory X is the style that predominated in business after the mechanistic system of scientific management had swept everything before it in the first few decades of the 20th century.

Theory Y is a participative style of management which "assumes that people will exercise self-direction and self-control in the achievement of organisational objectives to the degree that they are committed to those objectives". It is management's main task in such a system to maximise that commitment.

Theory X assumes that individuals are base, work-shy and constantly in need of a good prod. It always has a ready-made excuse for failure—the innate limitations of all human resources. Theory Y, however, assumes that individuals go to work of their own accord, because work is the only way in which they have a chance of satisfying their (high-level) need for achievement and self-respect. People will work without prodding; it has been their fate since Adam and Eve were banished from the Garden of Eden.

Theory Y gives management no easy excuses for failure. It challenges them "to innovate, to discover new ways of organising and directing human effort, even though we recognise that the perfect organisation, like the perfect vacuum, is practically out of reach". McGregor urged companies to adopt Theory Y. Only it, he believed, could motivate human beings to the highest levels of achievement. Theory X merely satisfied their lower-level physical needs and could not hope to be as productive. "Man is a wanting animal," wrote McGregor, "as soon as one of his needs is satisfied another appears in its place." (66)

Contrasting the theories

Table 7 summarises and contrasts the two styles.

Table 7. Theory X and Theory Y compared.

Aspect	Theory X	Theory Y
Work	Dislike	Like
Motivation	External	Intrinsic
Creativity	Low	High
Change	Resist	Embrace
Responsibility	Avoid	Seek and accept
Supervision needed	Maximal	Minimal
Management layers	Many	Few
Leadership	Centralised	Decentralised
Involvement in decision making	Low	High

Y over X

I spoke earlier in the introduction to this book about the findings from several studies that *people* with the Agile Mindset were the key to success, and that *process* ranked somewhere between being of secondary importance and being almost irrelevant. When it comes to the relationship between people and process, the theories are polar opposites.

Theory X values process ahead of people. Theory Y values people ahead of the process.

So it should come as no surprise that the Agile Mindset is based on Theory Y thinking. The Agile Mindset sees people as highly creative, intrinsically motivated with high involvement in decision making and a low need for supervision.

This is why one of the twelve Agile principles states:

Build projects around motivated individuals. Give them the environment and support they need, and trust them to get the job done.

In other words, get some good people together, give them a broad outline of your goal, and then get out of their way and let them do their stuff. Or as Steve Jobs once put it:

It doesn't make sense to hire smart people and then tell them what to do; we hire smart people so they can tell us what to do.

Now at this point you might be thinking something like *hold on a minute, what about this person I worked with at my last company. They were lazy, unmotivated and wouldn't do anything even when they were heavily supervised.*

Periodically we all come across people in Agile teams who seem to be highly Theory X and these people can appear to oppose McGregor's work. Thankfully one day at an Agile conference, a fellow attendee let me in on what I now refer to as the "McGregor's Secret Sauce".

McGregor's Secret Sauce

The (largely unspoken) key to Theory X and Theory Y is quite simply this:

Theory X and Theory Y are self-fulfilling prophecies.

Maybe take a minute and let that sink in. Effectively he was saying that the way you treat people, determines (to a large extent) the behaviours they exhibit. There is a cause and effect relationship between treating people as being a certain way (e.g. Theory Y) and them acting in that same way. In the Agile Mindset we believe that people generally will behave according to Theory Y when they are given the opportunity to do so.

For me, this was the missing piece of the puzzle. I'll grant you that there are some people who will probably be *X'ers* until the day they die, but the vast majority will respond positively when treated as though they are Theory Y people. This mindset is also a variation on Dweck's Growth v Fixed mindset we discussed earlier. If you acknowledge that people aren't fixed, and that they have growth potential, then you can also see that treating them in certain (Theory Y) ways can elicit growth behaviours that do not emerge in a Theory X environment.

People Over Process

When you hand good people possibility, they do great things.

—Biz Stone (co-founder of Twitter)

It is often said that culture eats strategy for breakfast. If this is true, then it could also be said that *people* eats *process* for lunch and dinner. Which is possibly why highly rated Deloitte CEO Cathy Engelbert condenses her leadership strategy down to one sentence:

Prioritize people over tasks

People are key to any endeavour. People have requirements, people write software code, people build things, people use the end product or service. Process and tools are only there to assist people to get the job done. Which is why the first value of the Agile Manifesto is worth repeating:

Individuals and interactions over processes and tools.

Most of us have seen this many times before. But what does it really mean? Have we stopped to consider *why* we should value people over process? And why do many organisations still seem to place so much focus on process? Let us see if we can answer these important questions. But first let's see what visionary former Apple CEO Steve Jobs had to say about people versus process.

Steve Jobs on Process

In his famous 1995 "lost interview", Steve Jobs spoke candidly on a number of subject including process and the how over time organisations build to a misguided level of faith in their processes. Although he mentions *content* several times, he is not referring to content as found in a document or a web page, but instead the content of the business – the culture, creativity and knowledge.

Steve Jobs: *You know what it is? People get confused. Companies get confused. When they start getting bigger they want to replicate their original success. And they start to think that somehow there is some magic in the process of how that success was created. So they start to institutionalise the process across the company. But before very long people get confused and think that the process is the content. And that was ultimately the downfall of IBM. IBM had the best process people in the world but they forgot about the content. And that's what happened a little bit at Apple too. We had a lot of people who were great at management process and they didn't have a clue as to the content. And in my career I found that the best people are the ones who understand the content. They are a pain the butt to manage. You put up with it because they are so great in the content. And that's what makes a great product. It is not process. It is content*

Heavyweight processes

For decades, following the legacy of Frederick Taylor, many organisations sought to develop processes that workers could follow to produce superior and repeatable results. The plan was to take people out of the equation and have them operate like machines. The need for repeatable processes was still a hot topic in the 1990's as it featured heavily in Michael E. Gerber's popular book The E-Myth, which suggested that implementing repeatable processes was a key component in enabling entrepreneurs to grow their businesses. And while there is still some value in this focus on process, it is becoming less relevant for the increasing number of knowledge workers who operate in an increasingly VUCA world.

In the early days of mechanization, factories and production lines these processes were extremely useful. It was only natural therefore that these types of approaches were applied to the early days of software development; projects and problems which at the time would have seemed intensely difficult but nowadays would be viewed as somewhat trivial.

But as processes grew and became larger and more complex, more deviations were encountered, more exceptions and edge cases were found. Processes then had to become even more complex and convoluted to cover all these eventualities. But then the problems we faced got even more complex, and a kind of insidious loop was born. Eventually, organizations would periodically reach a point of exasperation with their heavily mutated processes, and then finally switch to a nirvana solution in the form of another brand new heavyweight process which would function perfectly for a period of time up until the first deviation was encountered.

Lightweight processes

Agile processes, by contrast, are intentionally lightweight by design. They are designed to provide broad operating frameworks within which people and teams have a fair amount of "wiggle room" to tailor the process to the situation at hand. The processes can be altered to fit the people, not the other way around.

What do we mean by lightweight process? Consider these examples:

- The Agile Manifesto contains four values and 12 principles which can easily fit on a double-sided sheet of paper.

- The Scrum Guide is only 17 pages long.

Contrast this with the world's leading, and considerably more heavyweight, Project Management processes:

- The Project Management Institute's PMBOK Guide is 756 pages.

- The Prince2 guide "Managing Successful Projects with PRINCE2® 2017 Edition" is 400 pages.

This comparison above goes some way towards illustrating the difference between lightweight and heavyweight processes. Lightweight processes rely heavily on the people to adapt to the situation what face, whereas heavyweight processes are highly prescriptive and don't have that same reliance on people adapting the management process.

An interesting side note is that even predictive heavyweight PRINCE2® is designed to be tailored to some degree. The last of its seven principles is: Tailor To Suit The Project Environment, meaning that the process should not be followed in a dogmatic fashion but rather should be tailored to specific projects. However overall PRINCE2® would still be classified as a heavyweight process.

People-centric processes

You could be forgiven for thinking that all this talk about people over process means that we have no concern for the process at all. Nothing could be further from the truth.

A common mistake is to see the values in the Agile manifesto as saying we do one thing and not the other, when in fact they are saying that we value one thing more highly than we value the other. So when we say People and Interactions over Process and Tools it means that we value all of those things but we value the ones on the left, People and Iterations in this case, more than those on the right.

Processes are the ways we work together; the steps we take to get the job done. And they are crucial for getting people working together. The keys are to make the processes lightweight and adaptable as we have already discussed. For maximum success the processes should also be highly people-centric.

Organisations who focus on process leadership are often at a loss because they are focusing on repeatability and efficiency only. As we discussed earlier, today's pace of change in the market and in technology is unprecedented. Business leaders who are people-centered understand that a learning culture, tolerance for mistakes, and innovative approaches are required to thrive in this new environment. (67)

What determines a people-centric process? Firstly, the people involved are front and centre; the process should be designed to support the people doing the work, and not the other way around. Secondly the process should be defined with as much input as possible from the people doing the work, as they are the people with the most knowledge about the work being done. Lastly the process should be adaptable so that the people involved can adapt the work practices as they see fit to improve the process. As a bonus, acknowledging this last point can also take the pressure off having the get the process perfect the first time out of the gate; we can aim for a "good enough" first version of our process and then iterate, adapt and improve the process over time.

People as people

> We are not mere machines; we are human beings, and protest against being discussed and considered as coequal with machinery.

> -James Duncan, American Federation of Labor (AFL) officer, 1911

The heading for this section may seem trite. Treating people as people. After all, what else could we treat people as? Historically workers have been treated as anything but people, as resources, simply as cogs in a giant machine.

But people are not machines, we are human beings. We are diverse, complicated, error-prone, and sometimes irrational beings. We have good days and bad days, get on better with some people rather than others, have a unique mixture of personality traits, and individual preferences for how we communicate, think and work. Rather than pretend that people don't have these qualities, Agile works *with* these human qualities including the frailties and imperfections.

In this section we will look at how the attitude of people as resources still permeates a lot of organisations and explore what it really means to treat people as people.

Respect

Respect can be defined as the due regard for feelings, wishes, or right of others. It is the underpinning of the Golden Rule, a maxim that is found in many religions and cultures, "Treat others the way you want to be treated."

Historically respect hasn't played a large role in many organisational cultures. When you are operating under an authoritarian command and control structure you don't need to have much respect for the people below you, you just need to get them to do what you tell them.

A combination of factors including the rapidly changing operating environment, globalisation, the gig economy and flattening of management structures has meant that organisations now need to operate in a new way, and that new way is based on respecting individuals.

In July 2016 there was a small but very important update made to the official Scrum guide. Five values were added: Courage, Openness, Focus, Commitment and Respect. My reading is that Respect underpins all the other values. In a 2016 interview Scrum founders Ken Schwaber and Jeff Sutherland discussed why they added these values and highlighted the need for individuals, teams and organisations to really respect each other to be capable and independent individuals. Without respect, organisations can never move beyond the blame culture which has infected so many of them. (68)

In 2001, Toyota first summed up its philosophy and values calling it "The Toyota Way 2001". It consists of principles in two key areas: continuous improvement, and respect for people. (69). But the way that Toyota views respect is quite different from the way that many organisations think that they are showing respect. James P. Womack, Founder of the Lean Enterprise Institute, discussed the differences.

For many of us that doesn't sound much like respect for people. The manager after all doesn't just say "I trust you to solve the problem because I respect you. Do it your way and get on with it." And the manager isn't a morale booster, always saying, "Great job!" Instead the manager challenges the employees every step of the way, asking for more thought, more facts, and more discussion, when the employees just want to implement their favored solution.

Over time I've come to realize that this problem solving process is actually the highest form of respect. The manager is saying to the employees that the manager can't solve the problem alone, because the manager isn't close enough to the problem to know the facts. He or she truly respects the employees' knowledge and their dedication to finding the best answer. But the employees can't solve the problem alone either because they are often too close to the problem to see its context and they may refrain from asking tough questions about their own work. Only by showing mutual respect – each for the other and for each other's role – is it possible to solve problems, make work more satisfying, and move organizational performance to an ever higher level. (70)

Although there isn't a silver bullet to immediately turn your teams and organisations into highly respectful places, the book Agile Project Management for Dummies offers several ways to encourage respect. (71)

Foster openness. Respect and openness go hand in hand. Openness without respect causes resentment; openness with respect generates trust.

Encourage a positive work environment. Happy people tend to treat one another better. Encourage positivity, and respect will follow.

Seek out differences. Don't just tolerate differences; try to find them. The best solutions come from diverse opinions that have been considered and appropriately challenged.

Treat everyone on the team with the same degree of respect. All team members should be accorded the same respect, regardless of their role, level of experience, or immediate contribution. Encourage everyone to give his or her best.

Respect is such a crucial aspect of the Agile Mindset that success without a high level of respect is virtually impossible. And going hand-in-hand with respect is the need for trust.

Trust over control

We have already discussed trust as a primary underpinning for Psychological Safety. Trust is also crucial when we consider giving up control.

If, as the Agile Mindset suggests, we are to move away from the command and control methods which have been so prevalent historically, then it is imperative that we have high levels of trust. After all, how can we give up control to a team if we do not trust that team?

So are we saying no control at all? Not quite. Control remains part of the game, the difference is that it is practised differently. If I do not control how people do their job, what is it I control? The answer is "outcomes". As an agile manager, I can inspect (control) the resulting product increment at the end of an iteration. I have the opportunity to check (control) that it fulfils both feature needs and quality criteria agreed upon at the beginning of the iteration. (72)

Software maker Atlassian follows a similar ethos. While they have an internal playbook of best practices, they still let their teams solve problems to a large degree in whatever way they see fit. The corollary to this is that they measure everything possible so that they can keep tabs on progress.

And like its close partner respect, we don't have a sure-fire way of achieving trust. But we do have some sage advice about building trust from Patrick Lencioni's book *The Five Dysfunctions of a Team*.

As the manager, set the good example by asking for help from your team members, admitting your own weaknesses and limitations, and be the first to own up to a mistake. When you take the lead, others will follow. Slowly, these habits will become culture and the team will begin to build the first unshakable brick in the pyramid—trust. (34)

EQ over IQ

No discussion about people would be complete without discussing the importance of Emotional Intelligence (EQ). EQ is a term created by two researchers – Peter Salavoy and John Mayer – and popularized by Dan Goleman in his 1996 book of the same name. (73)

EQ is the ability to identify and manage your own emotions and the emotions of others. It is generally said to include three skills:

- emotional awareness;

- the ability to harness emotions and apply them to tasks like thinking and problem solving; and

- the ability to manage emotions, which includes regulating your own emotions and cheering up or calming down other people. (74)

Another way of thinking about EQ and IQ is in regards to problem solving:

IQ: The ability to solve problems that don't involve people.

EQ: The ability to solve problems that do involve people. (75)

Why is EQ such an important part of the Agile Mindset? Because Agile relies so heavily on teamwork and open, honest, and transparent communication both within the team and with other stakeholders outside of the team (76). As we work much more closely with both our team members and our stakeholders in Agile, we therefore need to have a much higher level of interpersonal skills than perhaps what was required when working under more linear, predictive methods.

We will look deeply into teamwork and collaboration in the next chapter but on an individual level EQ describes the skills needed to excel as a team member. Notice that we refer to the components of EQ as skills and not traits or attributes. This is because it is considered that EQ is a learnable skills that can be taught and improved upon, and not some sort of fixed inherent trait that we are born with.

According to Cornerstone University, EQ is characterised by 5 distinct characteristics:

1) Self Awareness

Those with high EQ are able to recognize emotions in the moment. One of the keys to developing EQ is being aware of feelings, evaluating those feelings and then managing them. Rather than letting emotions take over, you are able to take a step back and understand what is happening.

2) Self Regulation

Everyone knows that emotions come quickly and with force. It's rare that you have control over when we are hit by an emotional wave. Even the slightest thing can trigger something deep within you.

However, if you have a high EQ, you can control how long that negative experience lasts. This can be done by using various techniques (breathing, taking a walk, thinking positively) to minimize or effectively address negative emotions that may be plaguing you.

3) Motivation

It's very difficult to be motivated if you always have a negative attitude. Those who are full of negativity don't often achieve their goals. Those with a high EQ are able to move toward a consistently positive attitude by thinking more positively and being aware of negative thoughts. Reframing these negative thoughts allows you to be positive and thus move toward your goals.

4) Empathy

Empathy is the ability to recognize how others are feeling. This is essential for functioning well in society and excelling in your career. A person without empathy will end up regularly insulting and offending people, while a person with a high EQ will be able to understand what a person is feeling and then treat them accordingly.

5) Social Skills

The final characteristic of EQ is having and developing excellent interpersonal skills. It used to be that access to the greatest amount of information would allow you to succeed, but now that everyone has immediate access to knowledge, people skills are more important than ever. Those with high EQ are able to wisely and skillfully navigate the various relationships that fill their lives.

Research by Daniel Goleman shows that over 65% of all competencies deemed essential for high performance were related to EQ and that EQ mattered twice as much as IQ and technical knowledge for high performance. (77)

From the perspective of the Agile Mindset we can apply Goleman's research broadly in two areas. Firstly, we can place much more emphasis on EQ when hiring new starters. Some organisations embrace the motto that hard skills can be learnt a lot easier than soft skills, so they try to hire people who already have a high EQ. Secondly we can train our people to improve their EQ. Much research shows that EQ is a leant skill and training can improve individuals EQ and therefore improve their effectiveness when operating in an Agile environment.

T-shaped skills

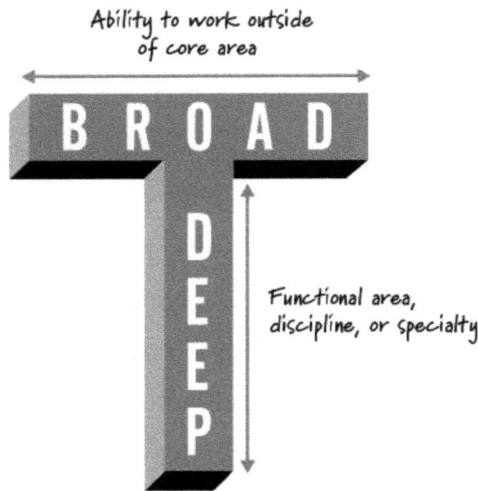

Ability to work outside
of core area

BROAD

DEEP

Functional area,
discipline, or specialty

Figure 19. T-shaped skills[6]

Let's finish up this section by discussing another important people aspect of the Agile Mindset; T-shaped skills.

T-shaped skills describe specific attributes of desirable workers. The vertical bar of the T refers to expert knowledge and experience in a particular area, while the top of the T refers to an ability to collaborate with experts in other disciplines and a willingness to use the knowledge gained from this collaboration. A t-shaped person is someone with t-shaped skills.

The concept of T-shaped skills was described by David Guest in 1991, but was popularised by Tim Brown, CEO of design firm IDEO, when describing the type of people he wanted to work for his organisation (78).

An example of a t-shaped skillset might be where a team member has one primary skill in accounting, and a number of secondary skills that they can pitch-in with when required e.g. social media, database administration.

People with T-shaped skills are often considered to be generalising specialist. T-shaped skills can be thought of as both a more accurate reflection on people and as an organisational goal for professional development.

There are several important points that are often missed in relation to T-shaped skills:

- Acknowledging T-shaped skills recognises that most people are multi-faceted, with many talents and does not put them in a box based on their role or job description. The mantra at some companies is "When we come to work we leave our job titles at the door".

- T-shaped people bring a multi-disciplinary approach to problem-solving that allows them to devise solutions which are outside of the mental models of the single-domain specialist.

- T-shaped people make excellent collaborators, and have already seen the importance that the Agile Mindset places on collaboration. Because a T-shaped employee has that broad experience at the top, she can collaborate cross-functionally like a boss. These people are not limited to skills and experience in one niche, but are able to contribute to a number of different projects and discussions that need attention (79).

- Not all work requires a specialist to perform the work to a satisfactory level. A specialising generalist can often produce work that is "good enough" to get the job done.

- Generalist animals (including humans) can be less efficient, yet they are less fragile amidst change (80). And we have discussed at some length how important it is to be able to adapt to the endless change that occurs in our VUCA world.

Summary

People are at the heart of Agile. The Agile Mindset is clearly a people-first approach built upon the values of respect and trust. It views people as creative, self-motivated and trustworthy human beings and not as cogs in a machine. It sees people as being more important to success than process and while processes are obviously still needed, they should be as lightweight and people-centric as possible. The Agile Mindset also values EQ over IQ and sees so-called "soft skills" such as empathy, emotional regulation and social skills as being qualities which align with Agile success. Lastly we should strive to build T-shaped skillsets in our people.

Key Points

- People are not resources, they are human beings and need to be treated as such.

- Treat people as though they are Theory Y and it will become a self-fulfilling prophecy.

- Emphasise People over Process

- Processes should be lightweight and people-centric

- Trust and Respect underpin the Agile Mindset

- EQ is valued over IQ

- Build and develop T-shaped skillsets.

Get your supplementary book resources from:
www.SchoolOfInnovation.net.

Key #6. Collaboration

> Alone we can do so little; together we can do so much
>
> -Helen Keller

In the previous chapter we looked at people and how they are viewed and valued through the lens of the Agile Mindset. Most of the work in Agile is done by teams of people working together (which is the definition of collaboration), rather than individuals operating on their own.

Organising people into teams is of course not something new, however historically collaboration has not always been a major priority; teams tended to work within silo's, customer contact for many teams was minimal and even within a team, the individual team members often focused solely on their individual task or area of expertise rather than working together.

The Agile Mindset places a high value on collaboration. Two of the four Agile principles concern collaboration:

- Individuals and interactions over processes and tools

- Customer collaboration over contract negotiation

And three of the Agile principles also focus on collaboration:

- Business people and developers must work together daily throughout the project.

- Build projects around motivated individuals. Give them the environment and support they need, and trust them to get the job done.

- The most efficient and effective method of conveying information to and within a development team is face-to-face conversation.

When we talk about collaboration in the Agile Mindset we are referring to more than just people working together. We are talking about achieving synergies amongst the team members which allows the team to make greater achievements than that which could have been achieved by the team members individually. The whole becomes greater than the sum of its parts.

Team success and achieving a collaborative state are not givens for any group of people. Collaboration does not necessarily just happen by itself and just throwing a group of people together does not make them collaborative. Collaboration often requires hard work and strong leadership. The key is that to get people working together rather than working as individuals, and in a mindset where they put the team first; success becomes a function of the team, rather than individuals within the team. Ownership and responsibility are shared by all members of the team.

Collaboration can also act as a guard-rail for overcoming any individual shortcomings that may exist within the team, and as a safeguard to mitigate any poor work practices that may arise unchecked when individuals are left to work on their own.

Collaboration has two close relations in coordination and cooperation. And while cooperation and coordination do play a part, collaboration goes beyond these two to a place where interdependence becomes the norm. One of the key differences between the three terms is that collaborations require high levels of trust whereas coordination and cooperation can occur without the same levels of trust.

There are three key behaviours which indicate a truly collaborative effort:

- Alignment towards shared goals

- Feedback through frequent two-way communication

- Shared accountability through consensus-made decisions

Agile Culture

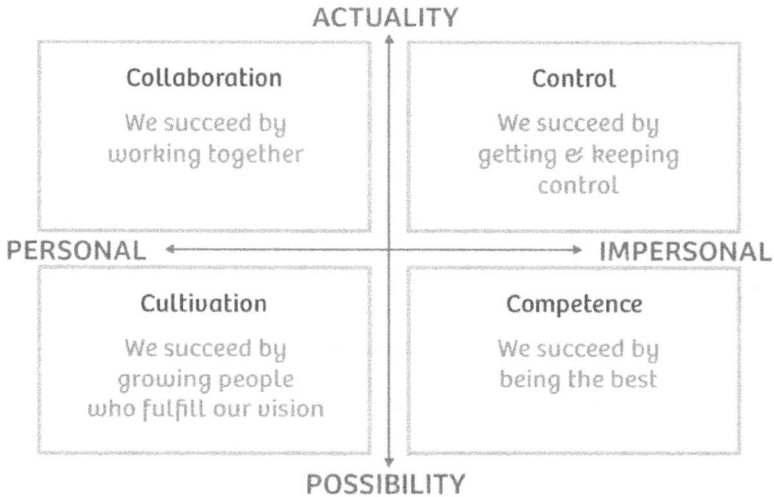

Figure 20. Schneider Culture Model (http://agilecoffee.com/toolkit/schneider-culture)

Another example of why collaboration is so important to Agile success can be gleaned from the Schneider Culture Model. Based on William Schneider's book *The Reengineering Alternative: A plan for making your current culture work* (81), the model provides a means of assessing an organisations culture and mapping where the culture needs to move to. Based on our understanding that Agile is a people-first mindset then clearly we need to aim for a culture high in either Collaboration and Cultivation.

Collaboration Everywhere

> The secret is to gang up on the problem, rather than each other.
>
> -Thomas Stallkamp

According to a salesforce.com survey, 86 percent of workers cite lack of collaboration and poor communication for workplace failures (82). So there appears to be a large need for better collaboration within organisations. The Agile Mindset is one which embodies collaboration everywhere; within the team, within the organization and with external customers.

Collaboration within the team

As mentioned earlier, two of the four values in the Agile Manifesto highlight the emphasis Agile methodologies place on strong collaboration. "Individuals and interactions over processes and tools" reminds us of the importance of strong and respectful communication. For example, rather than testers and developers using a defect tracking tool to record bugs, they are encouraged to sit and work together to recreate and resolve issues. "Customer collaboration over contract negotiation" reminds us that it's more important for a development team to allow for some flexibility to please a customer, seeking a collaborative solution to issues that might arise during product development, rather than to stick to a rigid contract (83).

On first viewing it might appear that every team of people is collaborating. After all, they are working together. And to a certain extent this may be true. However, scratch beneath the surface of many teams and you may find that they are only a group of individuals working in a coordinated manner. Team collaboration is not something that just happens automatically, it takes focus, the right mindset and strong leadership. One key step as we travel on the path towards collaboration is to start tearing down the walls which have siloed individual members within the team.

Tear down the wall(s)

The basis of collaboration is having a shared goal, a goal that the whole team is working towards. When you ask a team member what their role is, they should respond with the team goal rather than their individual role within the process e.g. test the software. This is in sharp contrast to the way that teams have historically worked, which has often been in an independent manner where tasks become each individual's responsibility rather than being the team's responsibility.

In this *siloed* approach, each role does their part of the process and then figuratively throws the work over the wall to the next role in the chain.

Contrast this with highly collaborative Agile teams, which exhibit a swarming type of behaviour, so-called because of the similarity to a bunch of swarming bees, where the team as a whole swarm together to attack one problem or task, and completes it, before collectively moving on to the next problem or task.

This type of behaviour is supported by having cross-functional teams – a team which has all the necessary skills to complete the task inside the team - and through the t-shaped skillsets we discussed earlier.

Another key attribute of a cross-functional team is that the team as a whole is responsible for delivering. Ownership and accountability are shared across the whole team rather than resting on the shoulders of one individual.

Collaboration within the organization

In the previous section we posed a simple test to identify whether team members are focused on the team's shared goals or on their own goals. A similar test can be applied to the organisation as a whole. Ask several members from different teams across the organisation to describe the company mission in five words. Do you get the same five words from each person across the different team? If not, then why not?

As important as a shared goal is for an individual team, a shared goal is at least equally important for an organisation. For the whole organisation to pull in the same direction, they first need to know what that direction is. The first step to creating a collaborative organisation is to agree and communicate the shared goal(s) to all members of the organisation.

The collaborative organisation mirrors the collaborative team in that all members see themselves as being on the same side and working towards the same shared goal(s).

The walls which may separate the individuals within a team can be mirrored by the departmental or functional silos within an organization. Functional areas within an organisation may have a long history of putting their own interests ahead of the organisation often due to reward structures and blame cultures. By employing the Agile Mindset we can break down these silos and allow our organisation to be more collaborative.

Cross-functional teams are a great way of removing the silos. Having a member from each silo in a team immediately breaks down many of those barriers. In addition to having organisation-wide shared goals, organisational accountability is another tool to enhance organisation collaboration.

Spotify Model

Moving beyond team collaboration, we start to get into different organisation structures such as the Spotify model of tribes, squads, chapters and guilds, as pictured in Figure 18.

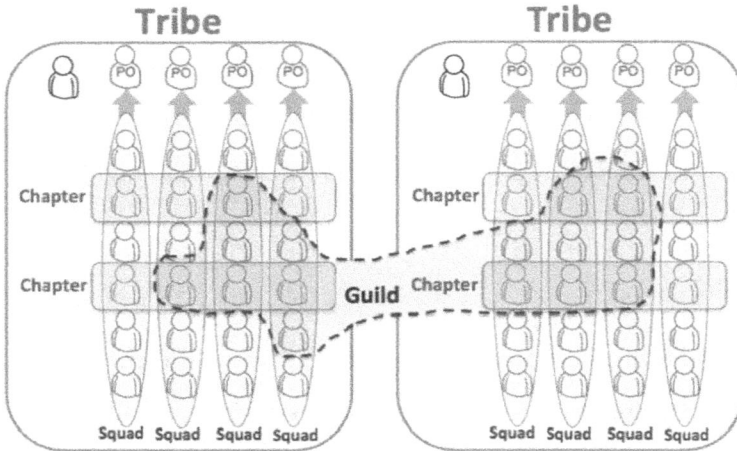

Figure 21. The Spotify model.

Spotify is quick to warn that they didn't develop this as a model per se, but rather it evolved over time to meet the needs of their organisation in solving their set of challenges. And while they don't promote their model as being something that should be copied by other organisations, because the structure embodies multiple threads of collaboration, it has been adopted by a number of organisations. Case in point is ANZ Bank in Australia which completely reorganised the company in line with this model into 150 tribes, or 150 start-ups as described by Christian Venter, General Manager of Technology and Digital Banking (84). Employees are joining squads, tribes and guilds based around shared goals and disciplines as the bank accelerates its transformation to a leaner and more responsive company (85).

Not all of this is new. Communities Of Practice (A Chapter or Guild in the Spotify model) have existed in organisations for many years, bringing practitioners of a certain role together to share information and increase learning. What is new is the formalisation of the model and the awareness of the value in collaborating across multiple dimensions.

While it is beyond the scope of this book to describe the Spotify model in full detail, I will draw on Emilia Barska's description (86) of the model's components to further highlight the multiple dimensions of collaboration which occur within this model.

A Squad – The Smallest Unit

A Squad is the smallest group of people, which is usually no bigger than eight members. They are responsible for one key area, such as maintenance, operations, design, tests, release, production. The Squad members have end-to-end responsibility and the team has one long-term task at a time. The freedom of their choices and decisions is limited by the company's mission and by the product strategy. The Product Owner decides on the hierarchy of priorities for Squad members. They are responsible for small and frequent releases.

A Tribe – The Grouped Squads

Squads work on similar tasks, such as solutions for smartphones, tablets, Apple or Android software. What all these squads have in common is they all work on mobile versions and this common factor makes a few squads a tribe. There are less than 100 people in each tribe. A Tribe Leader is responsible for managing tasks; however, this person is still a Squad member and has to fulfil everyday duties.

A Chapter – The Specialists

Each Squad has professionals who specialize in certain areas. All these people, who have the same responsibilities in separate Squads, are gathered in a group called a Chapter. A Chapter lead is a line manager here. Everyone is a member of both a Squad and Chapter.

A Guild – An Informal Structure

Spotify has a separate structure that allows their employers to gather according to their interests, tools, knowledge, etc. People from any Squad, Tribe and Chapter can join and leave anytime and, therefore, a lot of communities exist that have the power to integrate and share valuable knowledge. A Guild has a Guild Co-ordinator.

Collaboration with the customer

Historical project management approaches usually involve customers at only three key points:

- Project start: When the customer and the project manager negotiate contract details.

- Any time scope changes during the project: When the customer and the project manager negotiate changes to the contract.

- End of a project: When the project team delivers a completed product to the customer. If the product doesn't meet customer expectations, the project manager and the customer negotiate additional changes to the contract.

This historical focus on negotiation discourages potentially valuable customer input and can even create an adversarial relationship between customers and project teams. (87)

While contracts will always be needed, they are also often easy to hide behind by both parties. "They're going to hate it, but we're giving them exactly what the contract specifies.". (88)

The important value in the Agile Manifesto *Customer Collaboration over Contract Negotiation* is often overlooked. Rather than working in a combative relationship with the customer, the key mindset shift here is that the team and the customer should work together to achieve a shared outcome.

The aim of the Agile Mindset is for the customer and the team to work together in a partnership to deliver value. This is one of the reasons that many Agile practices include regular reviews or demonstrations of the work completed so as to engage the customer regularly as a partner in the build process.

Collaborative Leadership

As we look ahead into the next century, leaders will be those who empower others.

-Bill Gates

Many people struggle with leadership in Agile, largely due to having spent years or even decades under Taylorism-inspired management models. Under a command and control style of leadership the relationship is perhaps more straight forward; when the leader says "jump", the followers ask "how high". But in Agile we encounter new forms of leadership such as servant leadership and emergent leadership, and teams are largely self-organising with much less direction from above.

In this section we will unpack what Agile leadership looks like and discuss some of the leadership challenges that come with adopting this part of the Agile Mindset.

Servant leadership

With traditional leadership models, the image that often comes to mind is that of a pyramid, with the leader clearly at the top and the team below him. The leader is seen as the most powerful and best equipped to make decisions. Within this model the HiPPO (Highest Paid Person's Opinion) reigns supreme.

The model of servant leadership is a radically different model which flips the traditional pyramid upside down (Figure 19). Leaders are at the bottom of the pyramid and primarily tasked with supporting and enabling their teams. In this model a leader's success is based on how successful he makes those below him. The humility of the leader allows them to recognise that the best ideas can come from anywhere and often from those on the front lines.

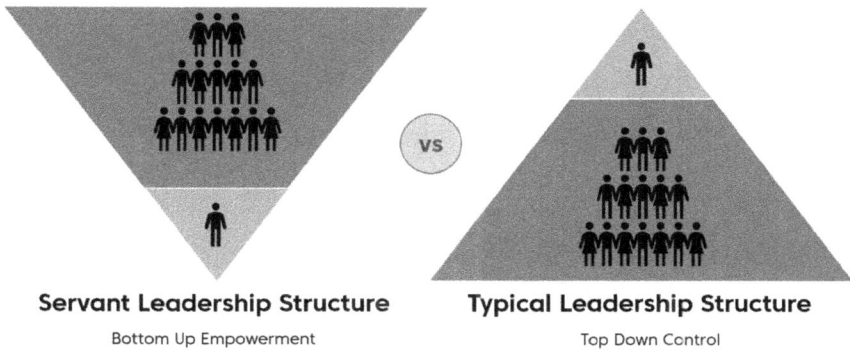

Servant Leadership Structure
Bottom Up Empowerment

vs

Typical Leadership Structure
Top Down Control

Figure 22. Servant Leadership compared to Typical Leadership

I find it useful to visualise it this way. If the team's goal was to produce a stage play, then picture the team at the end of the play. In the old leadership model the chances are that the leader would be the one at the front of the stage taking the bows and accepting all the applause. Under a servant leader, the team would be standing front and centre on a stage, directly in the limelight, taking bows and accepting the applause. The servant-leader will be standing behind them on the stage, or maybe even offstage out of view.

Servant leadership turns the traditional model on its head. It embodies the famous quote from Steve Jobs (which I will repeat):

It doesn't make sense to hire smart people and then tell them what to do; we hire smart people so they can tell us what to do.

The servant leader's role is to share power, put the needs of the team first, help develop individuals within the team, remove roadblocks and guide the team toward high performance.

Servant leadership is an ancient philosophy. There are passages that relate to servant leadership in the Tao Te Ching, attributed to Lao-Tzu, who is believed to have lived in China sometime between 570 BCE and 490 BCE:

The highest type of ruler is one of whose existence the people are barely aware. (89)

The phrase "servant leadership" was coined by Robert K. Greenleaf in The Servant as Leader, an essay that he first published in 1970. In that essay, Greenleaf said:

The servant-leader is servant first... It begins with the natural feeling that one wants to serve, to serve first. Then conscious choice brings one to aspire to lead. That person is sharply different from one who is leader first, perhaps because of the need to assuage an unusual power drive or to acquire material possessions... The leader-first and the servant-first are two extreme types. Between them there are shadings and blends that are part of the infinite variety of human nature.

Nowadays, servant leadership is advocated by some of the leading thinkers in management thinking including Ken Blanchard, Stephen Covey, Peter Senge, M. Scott Peck, Margaret Wheatley, Ann McGee-Cooper & Duane Trammell, Larry Spears, and Kent Keith (90).

Larry Spears identified a number of key principles in the writings of Greenleaf. These principles include:

- Listening
- Empathy
- Persuasion

- Conceptualization
- Commitment to the growth of others
- Building community

Servant leadership in the real world

Servant leadership seems like a nice idea but does it have legs in the real world? Yes, it does, and it can be found in some of the most unlikely of places.

In the US marines, arguably one of the best-trained defence forces in the world, the mantra they use is *Officers Eat Last*. Simon Sinek describes this phenomenon in his book *Leaders Eat Last*.

The title of the book "Leaders Eat Last" came from a conversation I actually had with a Marine it was a three-star general who's in charge of all Marine Corps training officer and enlisted and I asked him when I was talking to him a very simple question – what makes Marines so good at what they do? And he answered simply "officers eat last"

And if you visit any chow hall in any Marine base anywhere in the world what you will see when they eat at chow time is that all the Marines will line up in rank order. The most junior Marine will always eat first, the most senior Marine will always eat last. No order is given, there is no rule that says they will have to do this and nobody tells them they have to. It's one of the funny ways that it manifests when we see their perspective on leadership how it shows up – it's just one of the funny ways it shows up because they view leadership as a responsibility, not as a rank. It's not about being in charge it's about taking care of those in your charge. That's what leadership really is and the Marines embody it as a culture and it's sort of kind of amazing to see actually. (91)

From a very different sphere, we find that the All Blacks of New Zealand, the most successful Rugby Union team of all time and arguably the most successful international sporting team in any sporting code, have a long-standing tradition of the team's most senior players staying behind after the game to literally sweep out the sheds with brooms, in a gesture of humility and egalitarianism. (92)

When adopting the Agile Mindset we need to adopt servant leadership principles and train, or re-train, our leaders to operate under these principles. Only then can we truly put people first, and create an environment of trust, psychological safety and continuous learning.

Self-organisation

One of the 12 values in the Agile Manifesto states:

> *The best architectures, requirements, and designs emerge from self-organizing teams.*

At the simplest level, a self-organizing team is one that does not depend on or wait for a manager to assign work. Instead, these teams find their own work and manage the associated responsibilities and timelines (93). Such an organisational strategy is also known as a *Do-Ocracy* and is typified by people taking greater individual responsibility for solving problems and achieving goals (94).

Perhaps the best way to explain self-organisation is to compare it to two other common forms of organisation: manager-lead teams and self-governing teams.

Manager-led teams are the types of teams that organisations have typically used for many decades. Each team has a manager whom they report to, a person who needs to be included in most of the decisions and who directs the team and who should do the work and how it should be done. The manager is the boss of the team and reports along a hierarchical chain to the top of the organisation.

Self-governing teams are the polar opposite of manager-led teams. The teams are self-selected; formed organically by team members who find each other of their own accord. The team also decides on what tasks they will work on. They do not have any external manager or boss and are self-directed from within. While definitely in the minority, this type of organisation has been used for some successful companies including Valve (developer to the well-known Steam online gaming platform) and Gore (maker of waterproof, breathable fabric Gore-Tex).

Self-organisation sits somewhere between the previous two models. A self-organising team will often be given direction from outside but this takes the form a broad goal rather than specific instructions or directions. The team decides how they are going to reach that goal (the process), what tasks they will undertake and who within the team will do each task. (95)

Self-organizing teams are not free from management control. Management chooses for them what product to build or often chooses who will work on their project, but they are nonetheless self-organizing. Neither are they free from influence. Early references to Scrum were clear about this. In "The New New Product Development Game" from 1986, Takeuchi and Nonaka write that "subtle control is also consistent with the self-organizing character of project teams." (96)

Self-organization does not mean that workers instead of managers engineer an organization design. It does not mean letting people do whatever they want to do. It means that management commits to guiding the evolution of behaviours that emerge from the interaction of independent agents instead of specifying in advance what effective behaviour is. (97)

Emergent Leadership

Emergent leadership is closely aligned with self-organisation. Emergent leadership is a type of leadership in which a group member is not appointed or elected to the leadership role; rather, leadership develops over time as a result of the group's interaction.

Google in particular are big fans of emergent leadership and place a heavy weighting on this trait when hiring new employees. According to Laszlo Bock, former-senior vice president of people operations for Google:

Traditional leadership is, were you president of the chess club? Were you vice president of sales? How quickly did you get there? We don't care. What we care about is, when faced with a problem and you're a member of a team, do you, at the appropriate time, step in and lead. And just as critically, do you step back and stop leading, do you let someone else? Because what's critical to be an effective leader in this environment is you have to be willing to relinquish power. (52)

The key is that leaders emerge as the task on hand dictates. Perhaps someone with certain relevant skills or experience, or a drive to solve a specific problem, will step up to take a lead role for a period of time. Equally important is that the leadership can and will change over time as circumstances dictate.

High Performing Teams

> None of us is as smart as all of us.
>
> -Ken Blanchard

In Agile the focus is on the team rather than any one individual. Likewise, when it comes to performance we are most interested in building high-performance teams rather than high-performing individuals per se.

Many organisations have been searching for the nirvana of high performing teams for quite some time. But perhaps the formula is not so elusive as consulting firm McKinsey & Co discovered in interviewing over 5000 executives over more than a decade.

The results are remarkably consistent and reveal three key dimensions of great teamwork. The first is alignment on direction, where there is a shared belief about what the company is striving toward and the role of the team in getting there. The second is high-quality interaction, characterized by trust, open communication, and a willingness to embrace conflict. The third is a strong sense of renewal, meaning an environment in which team members are energized because they feel they can take risks, innovate, learn from outside ideas, and achieve something that matters—often against the odds. (98)

Viewing this through a different lens, Ricci and Weiss suggested that high performing teams are recognisable by ten characteristics:

- People have solid and deep trust in each other and in the team's purpose — they feel free to express feelings and ideas.

- Everybody is working toward the same goals.

- Team members are clear on how to work together and how to accomplish tasks.

- Everyone understands both team and individual performance goals and knows what is expected.

- Team members actively diffuse tension and friction in a relaxed and informal atmosphere.

- The team engages in extensive discussion, and everyone gets a chance to contribute — even the introverts.

- Disagreement is viewed as a good thing and conflicts are managed. Criticism is constructive and is oriented toward problem-solving and removing obstacles.

- The team makes decisions when there is natural agreement — in the cases where agreement is elusive, a decision is made by the team lead or executive sponsor, after which little second-guessing occurs.

- Each team member carries his or her own weight and respects the team processes and other members.

- The leadership of the team shifts from time to time, as appropriate, to drive results. No individual members are more important than the team. (99)

Tuckman model

Bruce Tuckman's Model of Team Development identifies a set of stages (Forming, Storming, Norming, and Performing) that teams need to pass through on to high performance (Performing = High Performing). Later on, Tuckman added a fifth stage called Adjourning to represent the increasing frequency of teams disbanding post-project completion.

Stefan Luyten provides the following concise descriptions of each stage:

Forming: the team is formed and team members interact on a very formal basis. They avoid conflict and are exploring each other's personality from a far distance.

Storming: the natural working styles of the team members clash and the first conflicts arise. This is the stage where people try to take important positions in the team and where the existing authority is questioned.

Norming: Emotions settle down and every individual personality takes its place in the team, differences are resolved and the team members' individual strengths are starting to complement each other.

Performing: This is the stage you'd want your team to be in. Performance is at its peak and the team is collectively, efficiently and effectively working towards a common goal.

Adjourning: The team is disbanded … celebrate its success and achievements! (100)

The Tuckman model recognizes that teams go through an evolutionary growth process. We cannot new expect teams to be high-performing from day one. The best that we can aim for is to shorten the journey to high performance through aligning the team on a shared goal, and creating an open environment based on trust where constructive disagreement can take place.

The model also highlights the need for different leadership behaviours as teams move through the different stages. Many people have blended the Tuckman Model with the Hersey/Blanchard Situational Leadership approach, to identify the preferred leadership approach at each stage of team development. (101)

Vicky and Martin Webster have summarised (Table 8) the mapping of these two approaches. (102)

Table 8. Tuckman Model combined with Situational Leadership

	Forming	Storming	Norming	Performing
Objectives	Introductions Set objectives Communicate: tell Dealing with distractions	Resolve conflict Facilitate relationships Discuss team progress Communicate: sell Promote openness	Share decision-making responsibilities Develop team processes Communicate: consult Encourage learning	Coach team members Delegate responsibility Communicate: join Promote self-criticism Observe and support
Directing behaviour	High	High	Low	Low
Supporting behaviour	Low	High	High	Low
Focus	Individual tasks	Team relationships Working through differences	Team processes	Self development Self- direction

The Wisdom of Aristotle

Whichever way you look at it; Google has been one of the most successful companies of this century. But never one to rest on their laurels, and in the truest sense of Agile, Google continues to learn, to grow and to improve. In this vein, they undertook a two-year study, code-named Project Aristotle, across 180 of their teams to try and discover what made the perfect team. Their quest was to identify the critical success factors which resulted in the highest-performing teams. (103)

We came across this study earlier in our discussion on Psychological Safety, which was far and away the most critical success factor. But there were also four other important factors which differentiated high-performing teams from the norm:

Dependability

Team members get things done on time and meet expectations.

Structure and clarity

High-performing teams have clear goals, and have well-defined roles within the group.

Meaning

The work has personal significance to each member.

Impact

The group believes their work is purposeful and positively impacts the greater good.

Along with Psychological Safety, these five traits can act as a powerful checklist and a signpost to how teams are progressing toward achieving high performance.

Collective Intelligence

While Google's Project Aristotle received a lot of exposure, a lesser-known study was undertaken by a group of researchers from several leading US universities. They set out to answer the question as to whether or not a group possessed its own intelligence? Was a synergistic group more intelligent than the sum of its members?

In short, their answer was Yes, that synergistic groups would outperform the sum of the individuals. However, they took their research a step further and discovered that how team members treated each other had a measurable impact on the team's performance. They identified two critical factors which contributed to this high performance:

Equal Voice - equality in distribution of conversational turn-taking.

Social Sensitivity - average social sensitivity of group members (social sensitivity is the ability to identify feelings in others).

Interestingly, these two factors contributed towards the collective intelligence of the group regardless of the average IQ of the group, nor the highest IQ in the group. As we discussed earlier, the Agile Mindset is all about EQ over IQ!

Summary

Collaboration underpins the Agile Mindset. The focus is on a team of people working closely together to achieve a goal. But collaboration extends outside the team to include new ways of working with customers and with the organization at large. Walls and silo's which previously separated individuals and teams must give way to cross-functional collective endeavours.

New styles of leadership are needed to operate in this highly collaborative environment. Teams are self-organising and exhibit transient emergent leadership where team members step up to take a leadership role as the situation requires and then retreat back to their equal team member position. While some external leadership is needed, this should be in the form of servant leadership where the leader's primary job is to empower the team to perform and improve.

All teams go through a natural evolution. The journey from forming through to high performing takes time but can be shortened by providing clear and meaningful shared goals for the team, and by creating an open and honest environment based on trust and respect, where team members can depend on each other.

Key Points

- The focus need to move from individuals working on their own goals, to teams working together towards a shared goal.

- Collaboration needs to occur within teams, across teams within the organisations, and with external customers. The goal is to gang up on the problem.

- Organisation silos can be broken down with cross-functional teams, communities of practice and guilds.

- All teams go through a natural evolution which can be shorted but not avoided altogether.

- High performing teams have a clearly defined set of characteristics, attitudes and behaviours.

- Servant leadership turns the traditional model on its head and the leader's primary role becomes to empower other teams.

- Humility is the defining leadership characteristic.

- Psychological Safety is the number one condition required for developing high-performing teams.

Download your free supplementary resources from www.SchoolOfInnovation.net.

Key #7. Value

Value is what you get, Price is what you pay.

-Warren Buffett

Many people think about Agile in terms of being able to deliver faster than they could before. While there is a speed element to Agile, there is a common misconception that Agile is primarily designed for speed. The key focus of Agile, the key orientation of Agile, is on delivering value.

The importance of value is not confined to the Agile world. Earned Value Management (EVM) has become increasingly popular in traditional Project Management methodologies since its creation by the US government in the 1960s. EVM is a project management technique for measuring project performance and progress in an objective manner (104). It tracks how a project is delivering value over time by analysing planned spending, actual spending, planned work completion and actual work completion. The importance of tracking value can be seen in The United States Office of Management and Budget mandating the use of EVM across all U.S. government agencies to manage programs and projects (105).

This focus on value emerged largely in response to the high number of abject project failures, projects where millions of dollars were spent and not one dollar of value was delivered (106).

Some notable examples of project failure include:

- Washington state's License Application Mitigation Project (LAMP) project. Begun in 1990 with a budget of $16 million over five years to automate the state's vehicle registration and license renewal processes. In 1997 the plug was pulled on LAMP, but not before seven years and roughly $US40 million had been wasted.

- In 2003 British supermarket giant Sainsbury's undertook a project to install an automated fulfillment system in its Waltham Point distribution center in Essex. The system promptly ran into what were then described as "horrendous" barcode-reading errors. In 2007 the entire project was scrapped, and Sainsbury's wrote off £150 million in IT costs.

- In 2000 the US Federal Bureau of Investigation (FBI) commenced a project to modernise their agile computer systems. Known as the Virtual Case File project, it was abandoned in 2005 after spending $170 million.

- In Germany they spent 15 years planning the Berlin Brandenburg Airport and started construction in 2006 with a target opening date was October 30th 2011. As of July 2018 the Berlin Airport has yet to open and now has a target opening date of sometime in 2020. The latest estimate of total project costs is €7.9 billion, almost 50 percent above the approved budget of €5.4 billion! (107)

From these examples where can see the truism in Warren Buffett's quote that we can surely pay a high price in return for very little value. We could spend a lot more time looking at project failures as there are so many of them, but the key takeaway is that initiatives can fail to deliver *any* value at all, and even projects that don't completely fail, often only deliver a small percentage of their promised value.

Part of the reason that many traditional projects have not delivered any value is that they have tended to be managed a way that delivers all their value at once, near to the end of the project. The Agile Mindset focuses on delivering value, and delivering that value early and consistently throughout the project, rather than waiting for delivery near to the end of the project.

Methods like EVM track the theoretical value of work being completed during a project. The problem with these methods is that the value being counted is often only theoretical value, and not necessarily realised value. Agile aims to actually deliver real live value and then only count this value once it is actually completed, deployed and being used. This focus, some might say obsession, of the Agile Mindset with value is based on the desire to avoid the types of abject project failure we saw earlier.

Value is most valuable

Our highest priority is to satisfy the customer through early and continuous delivery of valuable software.

-The Agile Manifesto

We took a brief look at some major project failures. They were failures in the sense that they didn't deliver *any* value at all, but did manage to use up a lot of resources. But what actually is this thing called value, who defines it and how do we get it?

Value is something of an abstract term. It represents a weighted combination of factors including effort, cost, duration, return and so on. Furthermore, value in Agile is seen as being fluid, relative and changing. Something that represents high value right now, may not have been of high value previously, and may not still represent high value at some point in the future.

Various Agile methodologies use different ways of determining value. Some organisations like to take a mathematical approach and use standard formulas such as IRR (Internal Rate of Return) or NPV (Net Present Value), or use custom formulas with various weightings to factors such as price, risk and cost of delay to determine which work will provide the highest value.

Other methods use a more heuristic or *gut-feel* approach. The Product Owner role in Scrum often follows this type of approach. The Product Owner is the person with both the budgetary control and the full authority to make decisions, and they themselves determine what has the highest value. They balance out the time, cost, urgency and a multitude of other variables (such as Return on Investment(ROI), Customer satisfaction, the effect on Net Promoter Score) and various stakeholders interests, to determine what is the most valuable work that an Agile team can deliver.

MoSCoW

A simple and common technique for sorting work in Agile is to use MoSCoW prioritization. In this method we categorise our work into one of four value categories:

- Must Have
- Should Have
- Could Have
- Won't Have (this time)

After sorting our work into the four categories, we then focus our efforts solely on *Must Haves* as these represent the highest value.

Regardless of the way we determine value, it is an essential part of the Agile Mindset to determine the highest value work and deliver that highest-value work first. And we must also continually make periodic reviews of our priorities to assess whether the relative values have changed. This is how we optimise for value creation.

Optimise for Value Creation

> Strive not to be a success, but rather to be of value.
>
> Albert Einstein

There are many different goals that we can optimise a process for. We could optimise for the lowest cost, highest speed or greatest flexibility. In Agile, we optimize for *value creation.*

Consider that you had a number of tasks that you wanted to complete and your team were trying to decide which order to complete the tasks in. There are several ways that you could sort or order the tasks. You could:

- sort the tasks by estimated duration and aim to do the quickest tasks first.
- sort the tasks by cost and do the cheapest tasks first.
- sort the tasks by difficulty and do the easiest tasks first.

You can probably think of other ways of sorting the tasks as well.

In Agile we sort the tasks by value and do the highest value items first. In Agile, *Value* is seen as the most valuable commodity.

This might seem straight forward, but an unfortunately extremely common anti-pattern is for Agile teams and individuals to still focus on what is commonly known as the *low-hanging fruit* – the things they can deliver quickly and easily rather than what is most valuable.

In the software development world, it is very common for everyone from programmers through to project directors to try and "just fix a few small defects" in lieu of working on the highest value work. Even though the defects may be a very low priority, quite possibly so low that they will never get resolved, there seems to be some sort of almost irresistible false economy to be achieved by completing a few easy tasks which have little or no relative value.

Timeboxing

One of the ways that we optimize for value in Agile is through the use of *timeboxes*. A timebox is simply a rigidly-enforced time limit on an activity, for example limiting a meeting to a 15-minute duration.

Those of you who are familiar with Scrum might recognize that every meeting in Scrum is timeboxed to a certain duration. What you may not realise is that the timebox is an artificial constraint, deliberately introduced to force the highest value items to come into focus.

When a team is having a timeboxed 15-minute meeting, the time restriction becomes the incentive to discuss the most important topics first, and avoid wasting time on lower priority topics at the risk of running out of time. If the meeting wasn't timeboxed, then it would be possible to waste much time discussing low-value items, time that would be better spent discussing, or working on, the highest value items.

Value Driven Delivery

This value-orientated approach is often called *Value Driven Delivery (VDD)*. In the approach, customer value is the key motivator (driver) behind all our actions, and our aim to is deliver the highest value in the shortest time. VDD can also mean that at times we may favour the *effectiveness* of delighting the customer ahead of the *efficiency* of keeping resources fully utilised (for example on low-value work).

Our focus on delivering the highest value first, often takes the form of an MVP.

Minimum Viable Product (MVP)

Minimum Viable Product (MVP) has two different meanings.

When most people refer to MVP today they are taking about the first version or release of a product. The product will probably be quite low on functionality but it still a full-blown product that can or will be released, rather than some sort of mock-up or model.

The other definition of MVP came from Eric Ries' Lean Startup movement and referred to the minimum amount of effort necessary to validate a hypothesis for a new product or service. Often this means using drawings, making paper mock-ups of products, just enough of something to show the concept to people in order to get feedback.

Whether you consider MVP to be the popularised concept, or that from the Lean Startup movement, consider what you would put into a MVP? You are going to want to put in the most *valuable* features. Your first release of a product should contain what is deemed most valuable for the users. There would seem to be little point in building a first version of a product which only contained trivial features.

Deliver Value Frequently

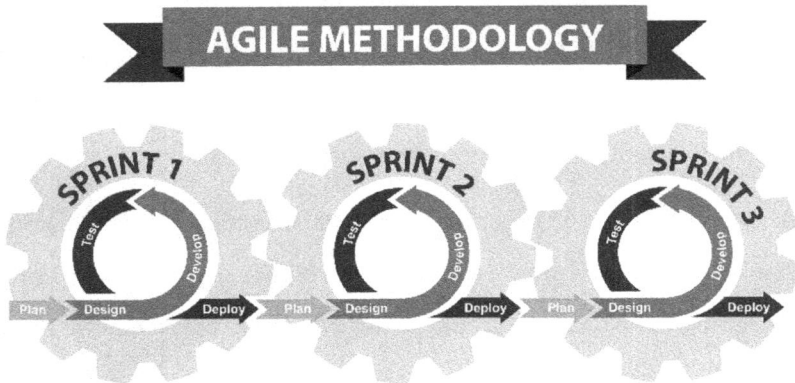

Figure 23. Agile methodology deliver value early and often.

We looked earlier at several monumental project failures. Many of these types of project failures are at least partly due to the idea of a *Big Bang* delivery, named after the cosmological *Big Bang* model for the creation of the universe in which the universe was created in an instance with a big bang i.e. it went from nothing to everything all at once. Projects delivery is named *Big Bang* when it tries to deliver all of their features at once, and normally near the end of the project.

The Agile Mindset sees this approach as inherently risky and turns the model upside down. It takes an alternative approach where it aims to deliver small slices of working product on a regular basis, for example at the end of every iteration (Figure 20).

This makes value creation highly visible, incremental and continuous. It also comes with two free bonuses.

Firstly, at the end of each increment there is a chance to get customer feedback, not just to verify that we have built to the specification but to validate what we have built actually meets the needs of the customer i.e. is the product fit for purpose.

Secondly, delivering value frequently has built-in risk management. As we showcase working value at the end of each increment, issues and risks are surfaced quickly where they can be dealt with early on rather than remaining hidden until late in the project.

Eliminate anti-value

> The most dangerous kind of waste is the waste we do not recognize.
>
> -Shigeo Shingo

You may not recognise the name Shigeo Shingo from the quote above. He was a Japanese industrial engineer who is considered as the world's leading expert on manufacturing practices and the Toyota Production System (TPS).

TPS was a precursor to Lean Manufacturing, often referred to simply as Lean. TPS introduced or popularised numerous key concepts which underlie many Agile principles and practices including Just in Time, Kanban boards and Kaizen (continuous improvement). TPS also introduced the concept of Muda (eliminate waste).

Waste

It has been said that the goal of Lean is simply to spend more of your time creating value for customers by reducing or eliminating everything else - the waste.

The Agile Mindset takes a similar approach, it sees waste as being anti-value and therefore an incredibly powerful way to increase value is to simply decrease anti-value, or waste.

Types of Waste

According to TPS there are eight types of waste that we should aim to eliminate:

1. Waste of overproduction

2. Waste of time on hand

3. Waste of transportation

4. Waste of processing itself

5. Waste of stock at hand

6. Waste of movement

7. Waste of making defective products

8. Waste of underutilized workers (108)

Elimination of waste is not a once-off activity. Rather it is an ongoing process. As things changes, as the team evolves, be aware that old practices which may have been ideal at the time, can become wasteful and may need to be modified or discarded.

Common sources of waste

Some readers may find the Muda's from the previous section to be a too vague to be useful, so to enhance your understanding I have included some examples of real-world waste from Maggie Millard. (109)

Defects/Mistakes

- Software with bugs that has to be re-coded

- Misdiagnoses in healthcare that lead to unnecessary tests or treatment

- Products that are shipped to the wrong address

- Manufactured items that don't meet the customer's specifications

Waiting

- QA engineers waiting for code to be developed

- Emergency room patients waiting for test results

- Landscapers waiting for the soil to be delivered

- Aeroplanes waiting for a gate to open up

Transportation

- Sending unsold products from the store back to the warehouse

- Ordering parts or products from distant suppliers when closer options are available

- Moving patients from one department to another in a hospital

- Moving equipment from one construction site to another

Motion

- Software that requires ten clicks to get to the screen you want
- Workers searching for missing tools or office supplies
- Printers and other equipment that are not conveniently located
- Inadequately stocked examination rooms

Overproduction

- Huge meals in restaurants
- Hospitals with more beds than the community needs
- Commuter trains with more cars than necessary
- Overstaffed retail stores

Inventory

- Shelves of unused office supplies
- Too much bedside equipment in a hospital
- Stacks of promotional literature or pre-printed forms
- Perishable items that will go bad before they are used or sold

Over-processing

- Software features that no one ever uses*
- An MRI when an X-ray would suffice
- Identical data that is entered in more than one place on the form in a software tool
- Complex purchasing processes with multiple approval levels

Human Potential

- Time is spent correcting errors or responding to emergencies

- Employees do not have the opportunity to learn new skills or utilize hidden ones

- Employees are not involved in process improvement

- Workers are not given a chance to advance within the company

*research by the Standish Group found that up to 60% of software features are hardly ever used. (110)

Context Switching

I will add one more important source of waste to the list and that is *context switching*. Context Switching is the activity of moving from one task to another task. The waste is introduced when we have not finished the first task and then have to pause that task, switch context to the second task, hopefully complete that task, then switch context back to the first task and pick up from where we left off.

Anyone who has worked in an open-plan office will have experienced context switching on a regular basis due to the constant interruptions which typify such an environment. Research has shown that for example, the average IT worker is interrupted every 15 minutes, which equates to 2000+ interruptions within a two-week iteration (111). That adds up to a lot of context switching, and potentially much waste.

In Lean Manufacturing, context switching is seen as a major source of waste and one to be avoided at almost all costs. Applying this to knowledge work, the key actions to avoid context switching are to:

- complete one task before starting another task
- minimize interruptions as much as possible

Building Unused Features

We have seen that there certainly are many ways to waste time and resources! As pointed out earlier, a key source of waste in software development is building features that are hardly used or even never used. The Agile Mindset has an approach to solving this problem called YAGNI.

YAGNI

YAGNI stands for **Y**ou **A**in't **G**onna **N**eed **I**t and is a mantra that comes from Extreme Programming (XP). It means that you shouldn't build things until you actually need them – until you absolutely, definitely, need them. XP co-founder Ron Jeffries has written: "Always implement things when you **actually** need them, never when you just **foresee** that you need them."

In Lean Manufacturing this approach is called Just In Time (JIT) and means that we should leave starting work on something, or making a decision, until the latest possible moment. The JIT approach present three key benefits:

- We don't waste effort on things that might look like they are needed now but may not actually be needed in the future.

- JIT can reduce Work In Progress (WIP).

- By leaving things as late as possible, we allow for the maximum amount of change and subsequent adaption.

YAGNI has a two cousins that we should also be aware of; Gold-plating and DTSTTCPW.

Gold-plating refers to adding features that the customer has not asked for, and is something to be avoided. We should ensure that we are only add features that the customer actually wants, rather than features we think they may want now, or in the future. Gold-plating goes against the ethos of MVP, because adding superfluous features, by definition means that we are not producing the *Minimum* set of features required for an MVP.

DTSTTCPW (Do The Simplest Thing That Could Possibly Work) means we should implement the simplest solution (not necessarily the easiest) so as to avoid the waste of adding unnecessary complexity. The astute reader may recognise this as an implementation of Occam's Razor, the edict that all things being equal, the simplest solution is superior to the more complicated one.

#NoEstimates

No talk about Agile and waste would be complete without mentioning the #NoEstimates movement. #NoEstimates is a somewhat controversial movement within the software development industry which purports that granular estimation of tasks is largely a waste of time and therefore should not be undertaken.

What #noestimates proposes is simple. It says that the precision obtained doing estimations using story points and the precision obtained only counting the number of stories without estimating and making use of the past statistical data is very similar. If this is true, all the time making the estimates is waste. (112)

Before writing this off as some sort of anarchist movement, you should note that there is evidence from well-known consulting firm Thoughtworks (113) and others (114) that the time spent estimating individual User Stories is wasted and that simply counting the *number* of user stories is sufficient to plan work effectively.

#NoEstimates is a highly emotional topic with vocal proponents on both sides of the argument. While it appears that more conclusive research is needed to conclusively validate the underlying hypothesis, it is also clear that some people appear to be operating successfully using a #NoEstimates approach.

My main reason for including #NoEstimates is not to necessarily promote the movement, but rather to highlight that even ingrained practices, such as task estimation, may not be necessary and could actually be hidden waste in some scenarios. There should be no sacred cows when it comes to waste reduction, virtually everything should be up for consideration, experimentation and testing.

Planning

This discussion of waste reminds me of the famous quote by Helmuth von Moltke the Elder:

No battle plan ever survives contact with the enemy

The meaning of this quote is that even the most intricate plans become irrelevant as soon as you begin to put them in place. The Agile Mindset clearly considers that planning has its' limits. In eliminating waste, we might also want to consider how much of our planning activities are out of habit, or designed to give us a false sense of certainty, and how much of those planning activates are actually valuable. As with most things in life, the answer probably doesn't lie at one extreme or the other, but rather somewhere on the spectrum between the extremes.

Let's finish up this section by looking at another key facet of the Agile Mindset, the need to focus on Outcomes over Outputs.

Outcomes over output

There's an old management adage that "if you can't measure it, you can't manage it", and this goes a fair way to explaining the historical management obsession with reporting and analysing outputs. Activities such as extremely granular time recording and resource utilisation reporting (including that resource known as the employee) are still highly prominent in many organisations, and undoubtedly justified in many cases.

However, there is a groundswell of thought that focusing on outcomes, instead of focusing on outputs, will lead to superior results and increased customer satisfaction. Joshua Seiden, in his book *Outcomes Over Output* defines an outcome as a change in human behaviour that drives business results. Outcomes don't necessarily have anything to do with making stuff, writing software, working a certain number of hours or finishing a certain number of story points. Seiden makes the point that in an environment of increased uncertainty, which we identified in Chapter 2 as the conditions which are becoming increasingly prevalent, teams capabilities are increased when planning is based on outcomes, as this doesn't limit teams' agility in the same way that output-based planning does. (115).

The focus on outcomes, on delivering value for the customer, also helps to avoid another common anti-pattern, and that is focusing too much on Agile. Yes, you read that correctly. This pattern happens within organisations and with the Agile community at large.

I have seen many organisations start down the path of an Agile transformation only to get side-tracked by the transformation itself. They start to become heavily focused on doing <insert Agile methodology here> the correct way. Pragmatism gives way to dogma. Heated arguments break out about the right way to do activities. Bigoted factions may also develop around certain Agile practices and so-called Agile holy wars may take place between faction members.

The problem with all this, other than potentially being an incredible waste of time and effort, is that the focus goes on to the correct way of doing things, and off delivering value to the customer and. Agile is a means to an end, not the end itself! Focusing too much on the Agile process or methodology itself can distract from the goal of delivering superior outcomes to our customers.

We've looked at how the Agile Mindset is extremely focused on delivering value and eliminating its' antithesis waste. Now let's look at how we actually deliver that value.

Deliver Value

Until delivery, ideas are a cost to the organisation not a benefit. It is like buying a book that you never read.

-Kevin Jackson in an article *Soft Skill Patterns for Software Developers: The 'Learning from Unintended Failures' Pattern*

The title of this section may seem obvious or maybe even a little patronising on first reading. After all, what else would we do other than deliver value? As we alluded to earlier, organisations and teams can often get pulled in many different directions, and become side-tracked from their purpose, which is to deliver value. Deliver Value is meant as a mantra, a way to focus on two things. Firstly, to make sure that we are working on the most Valuable work, and secondly to make sure that we are actually Delivering the work - completing and implementing the work rather than just starting it, or completing it but not getting it into customers' hands.

Only Done has Value

In Agile we often talk about the concept of *Done*. The original purpose was that *Done* would be a shared definition for when our team's work is complete. So that everyone, the team, the customer and other stakeholders all have a shared understanding of what we mean when we say that something is *Done*. This avoids the messy situation where people have different definitions of *Done* and the miscommunication that follows in such situations. For example, if the customer thinks that *Done* means that something is implemented live in production, and the product team thinks that *Done* means tested but not deployed to production, then much confusion and unmet expectations will follow.

Done also has another meaning though. It is the point where work can be considered to be of value. This raises an interesting yet subtle point which many people miss, and one which we will explore next.

Figure 24. Kanban Board example.

The Kanban in Figure 21 represents a simple workflow with three stages: In Progress, Ready To Deploy and Approving. Tasks in the *To Do* column have not been started, and cards in the *Done* column are finished work. As tasks progress through our process they move from left to right across the board.

Work in Progress (WIP) refers to any tasks that are "in play" i.e. that are in any of the columns between To Do and Done.

Lean thinking focuses heavily on limiting WIP and especially on limiting WIP within particular columns/stages so as not to cause blockages in the workflow.

WIP is waste

But there is also another very important reason for limiting overall WIP and I believe that this is a key part of the Agile Mindset that many people miss completely. **WIP is waste!**

Let me explain. A task that has not been started has generally incurred minimal cost to date. A task that has reached Done has realised value. But for WIP, once a task has been started, every step and in the process adds more to the cost of the task, without delivering any realised value. Remember that value is only realised when a task reaches Done.

Perhaps a competitor releases a new product, we get taken over by another organisation, or a crucial team member contracts a severe illness. Any number of changes can cause the process to have to stop. And at such points any WIP represents effort expended for zero realised return.

A pragmatist may argue that the tasks will be completed at a later stage and is therefore not all waste. This is possible and does occur in some cases, although it typically incurs the additional overhead that comes from context switching away from and back to the task, that would not have happened if that work had been completed as part of the original flow.

But also remember that when a re-prioritisation occurs, there is no guarantee that the partially-completed work will remain at the top of the To Do list (backlog), or that is will **ever** make it back to the top of the list. This is a radical change from the mindset which views to priority list as fixed and unchanging. Remember that value is fluid and that we should continually expect change. The key is to limit WIP and to aim to complete what we start.

Done is never Done

At this point you may think that I am contradicting myself, but stay with me here. Previously we have talked about the need to get tasks to Done in order to realise value. And this is true on a task level.

At a higher level though, at a product level, even though a piece of work may be done, the product is seldom completely finished. The idea that we finish a project and then the product is in any sense finished is an outdated and fixed mindset way of thinking.

The Agile Mindset sees products as continuums which are constantly being tweaked, with new features, fixes and improvements. Rather than a project having a hard stop and having a finished product we have the concept of a "continuous beta" or "perpetual beta" where the product is never finished but continues to gather feedback from the customer, which results in product changes, which result in further feedback from customers and so on ad infinitum; The PDCA cycle in action and incorporates the move away from viewing work as *Projects* towards viewing work as *Values Streams*.

Perpetual beta is not meant to be an excuse for shoddy beta-grade work. Rather it is a representation of the mindset which views the product being developed as a system, an ecosystem, which is never finished in the same way that a city is never finished.

I will wrap up this section by discussing a topic that is dear to my heart; Cost of Delay.

Cost of Delay

Cost of Delay is "a way of communicating the impact of time on the outcomes we hope to achieve" (116). Cost Of Delay puts a price tag on time, it takes into consideration both value and urgency of work items.

Cost of Delay calculates a data value, known as CD3, for each work item. CD3 can be thought of as *cost* divided by *duration*, although in reality the calculations often involve calculus which is beyond the scope of our discussion here.

Once calculated, the CD3 values are then often used to prioritise the work items using a Weighted Shortest Job First (WSJF) scheduling algorithm The result is a prioritised list of work items (product backlog) ranked based on value and urgency.

There are two reasons that Cost of Delay is an important topic.

Firstly, while many people have heard about Cost Of Delay, it has been estimated the 85% of product managers do not actually know the Cost Of Delay for the products they are building (117). With such a low uptake, it would appear that actively performing Cost Of Delay calculations is an opportunity to radically improve the way that many product managers work.

Secondly, I have anecdotally experienced a widespread belief that not doing something (i.e. doing nothing) comes as no cost. There seems to be little awareness that we can be incurring and accumulating an invisible debt, or loss of value, by not taking action. Finance departments are partly to blame here as they tend to focus solely on actual or committed spending and pay little attention to accounting the costs of inaction or delay.

Calculating the Cost Of Delay is likely to be highly valuable for some projects and less valuable for others. However, keeping in mind the broader concept that inaction and delay can incur cost and decrease value, has the potential to improve almost any endeavour.

Summary

Agile is highly focused, maybe even obsessed, with delivering value, and for good reason. Some projects have been spectacular failures and one of the things many of them they had in common is that they calculated theoretical value throughout the project but only tried to deliver any realised value close to the end of the project. Agile takes the opposite view to this *Big Bang* approach. It aims to deliver realised value regularly and consistently in small increments throughout the project.

Lean thinking focuses heavily on eliminating various forms of waste. Waste is seen as anti-value and removing anti-value is considered the equivalent of adding value. Removing waste is an ongoing exercise and we need to remain aware that practices can change from valuable to wasteful over time.

Deliver Value is a good mantra for Agile teams to adopt and this focuses them on not only making sure that they are working on the most valuable work, but that they are also actually completing what they are working on. Only work that is completed can realise value and Work In Progress should be considered waste until it is Done. And lastly always take into consideration the cost of delay - the cost of inaction.

Keys Points

- Agile is optimized for delivering value

- Value in fluid, relative and changing.

- Increase value by eliminating anti-value (waste).

- Work In Progress (WIP) can be viewed as waste.

- Team's mantra should become *Deliver Value*.

- Only Done work realizes value.

- Explore the hidden negative value of Cost Of Delay.

- Eliminate waste and increase value by using MoSCoW, timeboxes, MVP, YAGNI and reducing content switching.

Get your free Agile Mindset resources at:
www.SchoolOfInnovation.net.

Unlocking the Agile Mindset

One's destination is never a place, but a new way of seeing things.

-Henry Miller

We have covered a lot of ground in this book and drawn on information from a wide variety of sources. We have looked at the Agile Mindset through several different perspectives and tried to draw a thread through those perspectives to tie them together. I hope that as you have progressed through this book that you have started to see the connections between the various perspectives and started to form a picture of the Agile Mindset as a whole.

You may have encountered some new ideas which don't sit comfortably with you yet. That is Ok. Give yourself time to adapt to these new ways of thinking. Try these ideas on like a piece of new clothing and shed any that don't work for you.

You may also disagree with some of the things that I've written. In which case I am happy for you, because in all likelihood your disagreement has allowed you to deepen your comprehension of some part of the Agile Mindset in a way that makes sense to you. Feel free to let me

Remember though that my goal here has not been to argue that the Agile Mindset is "correct" in any way, but rather to simply unlock what that mindset **is**, so that if you are on an Agile journey then you can greatly increase your chances of success by understanding the core thinking and philosophy behind it.

This book contains the keys, but it is now up to you to unlock the Agile Mindset for yourself. And how should you go about doing that? Well, perhaps not surprisingly, I am going to suggest that you should take an Agile approach! Set a clear vision and then focus on mastering one small area at a time, building incrementally until you achieve the level of mastery you desire.

In this chapter I'm going to provide two blueprints; one at a personal level, and one at an organization level, that you may wish to follow as your path journey to unlock the Agile Mindset. As with everything in Agile, feel free to modify as you see fit.

Personal Roadmap

1. Set a clear vision for your outcome.
2. Break the mindset down into manageable chunks
3. Spend time learning each chunk, one at a time. Use this books as a starting point but do your own research as well.
4. Develop ways of implementing the Agile Mindset in your day-to-day practice.
5. Don't be afraid to fail. Conduct fail-safe-to-fail experiments.
6. Journal your thoughts, learning and insights
7. Regularly reflect on your journey.
8. Continually learn and improve.

Organisational Roadmap

1. Recognise that there is a journey to get to the Agile Mindset and set realistic expectations accordingly.
2. Attain executive-level championing for the journey.
3. Socialise the new management mindset.
4. Align the rewards system in your organisation with the Agile Mindset. Move rewards from individuals to teams, and from departments to the organization as a whole.
5. Train, mentor and coach people within the organization.
6. Focus on a few critical shifts in behaviour. Don't try to change everything at once. Make Incremental progress
7. Don't be afraid to fail. Conduct fail-safe-to-fail experiments.
8. Create knowledge within the organization and allow everyone to contribute to that knowledge.

Handing over the keys

I wish you and your organisation the best of luck on your Agile journey. Please let me know if I can assist you in any way.

What Did You Think?

Thank you for purchasing **Unlocking the Agile Mindset**. I hope you have gained some valuable insights that will help improve your Agile ways of working.

Gaining exposure as an independent author relies mostly on word-of-mouth, so if you have the time and inclination, please consider leaving a short review wherever you can.

Many thanks!

Also by the same author

The Agile Meeting Toolkit: 100+ simple ways for Scrum Masters to energise Agile meetings and engage Agile teams

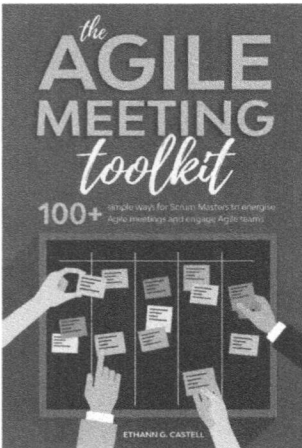

About the author

Ethann Castell is an Agile Educator, Coach, Author, Traveller, and the Creator of The School Of Innovation who has his sights on empowering companies to master the art of pragmatic agility. In addition to his relentless passion for all things agile and 20 years' worth of industry expertise, he holds an MBA and an array of certifications in the areas of Agile, Design Thinking, Training Design, and Delivery. To find out more about Ethann and his thriving education platform, visit his website at www.SchoolOfInnovation.net

Bibliography

1. The State of Agile Software in 2018. *MartinFowler.com*. [Online] 25 August 2018. [Cited: 7 July 2019.] https://martinfowler.com/articles/agile-aus-2018.html.

2. Hunt, Andy. Personal correspondence from Andy Hunt via Email. 2000.

3. Fowler, Martin. ShuHaRi. *martinfowler.com*. [Online] 22 August 2014. [Cited: 13 1 2018.] https://martinfowler.com/bliki/ShuHaRi.html.

4. *Computations of uncertainty mediate acute stress responses in humans.* Archy O. de Berker, Robb B. Rutledge, Christoph Mathys, Louise Marshall, Gemma F. Cross, Raymond J. Dolan & Sven Bestmann. s.l. : Nature Communications, 2016. 10996.

5. Konnikova, Maria. Why we need answers. *New Yorker*. [Online] 30 April 2013. [Cited: 17 10 2017.] https://www.newyorker.com/tech/elements/why-we-need-answers.

6. Rock, Dr David. A Hunger for Certainty. *Psychology Today*. [Online] 25 October 2009. [Cited: 14 February 2018.] https://www.psychologytoday.com/au/blog/your-brain-work/200910/hunger-certainty.

7. Staude, Miles. The value of 'value' and Benjamin Graham's three core beliefs. *Firstlinks*. [Online] 25 July 2019. [Cited: 27 July 2019.] https://www.firstlinks.com.au/value-benjamin-graham.

8. The perils of prediction. *The Economist*. May 31st, 2007.

9. Lehrer, Jonah. The Certainty Bias: A Potentially Dangerous Mental Flaw. *Scientific American*. [Online] [Cited: 28 March 2018.] https://www.scientificamerican.com/article/the-certainty-bias/.

10. Hfstede, Gert. The cultural relativity of organizational theories. *Journal ofInternational Business Studies*. 1983, Vol. XIV, 2.

11. Nyce, Caroline Mimbs. The Winter Getaway That Turned the Software World Upside Down. *The Atlantic*. [Online] 8 December 2017. [Cited: 13 June 2018.] https://www.theatlantic.com/technology/archive/2017/12/agile-manifesto-a-history/547715/.

12. Wai, Jonathan. The Growing Complexity of Everyday Life. *Psychology Today*. [Online] 12 November 2012. [Cited: 3 October 2017.] https://www.psychologytoday.com/au/blog/finding-the-next-einstein/201211/the-growing-complexity-everyday-life.

13. McGrath, Rita Gunther. The World Is More Complex than It Used to Be. *Harvard Business Review*. [Online] 31 August 2011. [Cited: 17 July 2017.] https://hbr.org/2011/08/the-world-really-is-more-compl.html.

14. Darrell K. Rigby, Jeff Sutherland and Hirotaka Takeuchi. Embracing Agile. *Harvard Business Review*. 2016, May.

15. Jeffrey Rubin, Dana Chisnell. *Handbook of Usability Testing: How to Plan, Design, and Conduct Effective Tests*. s.l. : Wiley, 2008. 978-0470185483.

16. Morris, Langdon. *The Innovation Master Plan*. s.l. : Innovation Academy, 2011. 978-0615512020.

17. Commoditization. *Wikipedia*. [Online] [Cited: 13 4 2018.] https://en.wikipedia.org/wiki/Commoditization.

18. Richard Dobbs, James Manyika, and Jonathan Woetzel. The four global forces breaking all the trends. *McKinsey & Company*. [Online] April 2015. https://www.mckinsey.com/business-functions/strategy-and-corporate-finance/our-insights/the-four-global-forces-breaking-all-the-trends.

19. Brown, Jessica. Is social media bad for you? *BBC*. [Online] 5 January 2018. [Cited: 15 March 2018.] http://www.bbc.com/future/story/20180104-is-social-media-bad-for-you-the-evidence-and-the-unknowns.

20. Weston, Charlie. Fail Hard. Fail Fast. Fail Often. *Medium*. [Online] 3 April 2017. [Cited: 14 June 2018.] https://medium.com/@rcweston/fail-hard-fail-fast-fail-often-3ca31180b988.

21. Agile Manifesto. *Agile Manifesto*. [Online] http://agilemanifesto.org/.

22. Company Values. *Atlassian*. [Online] https://www.atlassian.com/company/values.

23. White, Kye. Culture clash: What Atlassian did when they realised they had hired an 'arsehole'. *Smart Company*. [Online] 15 November 2015. [Cited: 10 December 2017.] https://www.smartcompany.com.au/people-human-resources/human-resources/culture-clash-what-atlassian-did-when-they-realised-they-had-hired-an-arsehole/.

24. Schwaber, Ken. *Agile Project Management with Scrum*. s.l. : Microsoft Press US, 2004. 978-0735619937.

25. Cook, Yoram (Jerry) R. Wind and Colin. *The Power of Impossible Thinking: Transform the Business of Your Life and the Life of Your Business.* s.l. : FT Press, 2006. 978-0131877283.

26. Schön, Donald. *The Reflective Practitioner: How professionals think in action.* London : Taylor & Francis Ltd, 1995. 9781857423198.

27. Contributor, Julie Chakraverty. Why embracing and discussing failure is good for your company culture. *Forbes.* [Online] Forbes, 3 December 2018. [Cited: 14 April 2019.] https://www.forbes.com/sites/voicesfromeurope/2018/12/03/why-embracing-and-discussing-failure-is-good-for-your-company-culture/#3317bd8d68ae.

28. Zimmerman, Eilene. Baba Shiv: Failure is the Mother of Innovation. *Insights by Stanford Business.* [Online] Stanford Graduate School of Business, 2 March 2016. [Cited: 19 February 2018.] https://www.gsb.stanford.edu/insights/baba-shiv-failure-mother-innovation.

29. Choi, Janet. Failure & Cake: A Guide to Spotify's Psychology of Success. *I Done This Blog.* [Online] 8 May 2014. [Cited: 17 April 2018.] http://blog.idonethis.com/spotify-growth-mindset/.

30. Rozovsky, Julia. The five keys to a successful Google team. *Google re:Work.* [Online] 17 November 2015. [Cited: 25 February 2018.] https://rework.withgoogle.com/blog/five-keys-to-a-successful-google-team.

31. Creating Psychological Safety in the Workplace. *Harvard Business Review.* [Online] 22 January 2019. [Cited: 19 September 2019.] https://hbr.org/ideacast/2019/01/creating-psychological-safety-in-the-workplace.

32. Snowden, Dave. Safe-to-Fail Probes. *Cognitive Edge.* [Online] [Cited: 12 June 2018.] http://cognitive-edge.com/methods/safe-to-fail-probes/.

33. Ledalla, Madhavi. TRUST – The Unspoken Element of Being Agile. *Apple Brook Consulting.* [Online] 1 May 2016. [Cited: 13 February 2018.] https://apple-brook.com/trust-the-unspoken-element-of-being-agile/.

34. Lencioni, Patrick. *The Five Dysfunctions of a Team.* s.l. : Jossey-Bass, 2002. ISBN-13: 978-0787960759.

35. David H. Maister, Robert Galford, Charles Green. Understanding The Trust Equation. *Trusted Advisor.* [Online] [Cited: 2 May 2018.] http://trustedadvisor.com/why-trust-matters/understanding-trust/understanding-the-trust-equation#top.

36. Davies, Rachel. Building Trust on Agile Teams. *Agile Coaching.* [Online] 3 August 2010. [Cited: 4 April 2019.] http://agilecoach.typepad.com/agile-coaching/2010/08/building-trust.html.

37. Levin, Marissa. 8 Ways to Build a Culture of Trust Based on Harvard's Neuroscience Research. *Inc.* [Online] 5 October 2017. [Cited: 15 5 2018.] https://www.inc.com/marissa-levin/harvard-neuroscience-research-reveals-8-ways-to-build-a-culture-of-trust.html.

38. Zak, Paul J. The Neuroscience of Trust. *Harvard Business Review.* [Online] January 2017. [Cited: 18 4 2018.] https://hbr.org/2017/01/the-neuroscience-of-trust.

39. Eriksson, Ulf. How Spotify does Agile – a look at the spotify engineering culture. *ReQTest Blog.* [Online] 31 March 2015. [Cited: 1 June 2018.] https://reqtest.com/agile-blog/how-spotify-does-agile-a-look-at-the-spotify-engineering-culture/.

40. Kanter, Beth. Go Ahead, Take a Failure Bow. *Harvard Business Review.* [Online] Harvard Business Review, 17 April 2013. [Cited: 18 August 2019.] https://hbr.org/2013/04/go-ahead-take-a-failure-bow.

41. Julie Hodges, Roger Gill. *Sustaining Change in Organizations.* London : SAGE Publications, 2015. p. 226. 1473911001.

42. Broza, Gil. *The Agile Mind-Set.* s.l. : Leanpub, 2016.

43. Brown, David. Here's what 'fail fast' really means. *Venture Beat.* [Online] 15 March 2015. [Cited: 13 June 2018.] https://venturebeat.com/2015/03/15/heres-what-fail-fast-really-means/.

44. Newman, Daniel. Secret To Digital Transformation Success: Fail Fast To Innovate Faster. *Forbes.* [Online] 16 May 2017. [Cited: 17 May 2018.] https://www.forbes.com/sites/danielnewman/2017/05/16/secret-to-digital-transformation-success-fail-fast-to-innovate-faster/#70642b806907.

45. Sims, Peter. *Little Bets: How Breakthrough Ideas Emerge from Small Discoveries.* s.l. : Simon & Schuster, 2013. 978-1439170434.

46. Goetz, Thomas. Harnessing the power of feedback loops. *Wired.* [Online] 19 June 2011. https://www.wired.com/2011/06/ff_feedbackloop/.

47. Ries, Eric. *The lean startup: how today's entrepreneurs use continuous innovation to create radically successful businesses.* s.l. : Crown publishing, 2014. p. 103. ISBN 9780307887894..

48. Dorf, Steve Blank and Bob. *The startup owner's manual: the step-by-step guide for building a great company.* Pescadero, CA : K&S Ranch, Inc, 2012. ISBN 9780984999309.

49. Zwilling, Marty. The Top 10 Ways Entrepreneurs Pivot A Lean Startup. *Business Insider.* [Online] 17 September 2011. https://www.businessinsider.com.au/top-10-ways-entrepreneurs-pivot-a-lean-startup-2011-9.

50. Continuous Learning: An Essential Strategy for your Personal Success. *Innovation Management.* [Online] http://www.innovationmanagement.se/imtool-articles/continuous-learning-an-essential-strategy-for-your-personal-success/.

51. Friday, Lucille Halloran and Catherine. *The University of the Future.* s.l. : EY, 2018. APAC no. AU00003263.

52. Friedman, By Thomas L. How to Get a Job at Google. *New York Times.* [Online] 14 February 2014. [Cited: 17 April 2018.] https://www.nytimes.com/2014/02/23/opinion/sunday/friedman-how-to-get-a-job-at-google.html.

53. What is Kaizen? *Kanbanchi blog.* [Online] https://www.kanbanchi.com/what-is-kaizen.

54. Byrne, Art. Kaizen Learning vs. Traditional Problem-Solving. *Lean Enterprise Institute.* [Online] 10 December 2015. https://www.lean.org/LeanPost/Posting.cfm?LeanPostId=512.

55. Palmer, Andrew. Lifelong learning is becoming an economic imperative. *The Economist.* [Online] 12 January 2017. [Cited: 17 June 2018.] https://www.economist.com/special-report/2017/01/12/lifelong-learning-is-becoming-an-economic-imperative.

56. Anthony, Scott. Kodak's Downfall Wasn't About Technology. *Harvard Business Review.* [Online] 15 July 2016. [Cited: 22 June 2018.] https://hbr.org/2016/07/kodaks-downfall-wasnt-about-technology.

57. Stephen J. Gill, Ph.D. Key Elements of a Learning Culture. *The Performance Improvement Blog.* [Online] 15 October 2013. http://stephenjgill.typepad.com/performance_improvement_b/2013/10/key-elements-of-a-learning-culture.html.

58. Bielicki, Przemysław. Seven Principles of Lean Software Development - Create Knowledge. *From Java to Java EE blog.* [Online] 7 January 2009. [Cited: 17 May 2018.] http://blog.bielu.com/2009/01/seven-principles-of-lean-software.html.

59. Alan Shalloway, Guy Beaver, and Jim Trott. *Lean-Agile Software Development: Achieving Enterprise Agility.* s.l. : Addison-Wesley Professional, 2009. ISBN-13: 978-0321532893.

60. OOSTERWAL, Dantar P. *The Lean Machine: How Harley-Davidson Drove Top-Line Growth and Profitability with Revolutionary Lean Product Development.* s.l. : Amacom, 2010. ISBN:9780814413791.

61. Poppendieck, Mary Poppendieck and Tom. *Implementing Lean Software Development.* s.l. : Addison-Wesley Professional, 2006. ISBN-13: 978-0321437389.

62. Traditional vs. Agile Project Management: Common Concepts with Different Implementations. *Agile PrepCast.* [Online] https://www.project-management-prepcast.com/free/pmi-acp-exam/articles/844-traditional-vs-agile-project-management-common-concepts-with-different-implementations.

63. Browning, Viktor Lev´ardy and Tyson R. An Adaptive Process Model to Support Product. *IEEE Transactions on Engineering Management.* 2009, Vol. 56, 4.

64. Fowler, Martin. The New Methodology. *MartinFowler.com.* [Online] 13 December 2005. https://www.martinfowler.com/articles/newMethodology.html#TheSelf-adaptiveProcess.

65. Pink, Daniel H. *Drive: The Surprising Truth About What Motivates Us.* Riverhead Books : s.n., 2011. 978-1594484803.

66. Theories X and Y. *The Economist.* [Online] 6 October 2008. [Cited: 13 November 2017.] https://www.economist.com/news/2008/10/06/theories-x-and-y.

67. Zwilling, Martin. Smart Entrepreneurs Favor People-Centric Leadership. *Huffington Post.* [Online] 17 April 2017. https://www.huffingtonpost.com/entry/smart-entrepreneurs-favor-people-centric-leadership_us_58f7e81ce4b081380af51896.

68. Sutherland, Ken Schwaber and Jeff. Scrum Guide Refresh July 2016 - Scrum Pulse Episode #14. s.l. : YouTube, July 2016.

69. Toyota. Environmental & Social Report 2003. *Toyota web site.* [Online] 2003. [Cited: 1 June 2018.] http://www.toyota.co.jp/en/environmental_rep/03/pdf/E_p80.pdf.

70. Womack, Jim. Respect for people. *Lean Enterprise Institute.* [Online] 20 December 2017. [Cited: 20 February 2018.] https://www.lean.org/womack/DisplayObject.cfm?o=755.

71. Mark C. Layton, Steven J. Ostermiller. *Agile Project Management For Dummies, 2nd Edition.* s.l. : Wiley, 2017. ISBN-13: 978-1119405696.

72. Building an agile mindset – Trust or control? *Novatec blog.* [Online] 23 August 2017. [Cited: 24 June 2018.] https://blog.novatec-gmbh.de/agile-mindset-trust-vs-control/.

73. What is Emotional Intelligence? *Institute for Health and Human Potential.* [Online] [Cited: 3 March 2018.] https://www.ihhp.com/meaning-of-emotional-intelligence.

74. Psychology Today. Emotional Intelligence. *Psychology Today.* [Online] [Cited: 13 March 2018.] https://www.psychologytoday.com/au/basics/emotional-intelligence.

75. Ward, Henry. IQ and EQ. *Medium.* [Online] 3 January 2017. [Cited: 7 August 2017.] https://medium.com/eshares-blog/iq-and-eq-cf540bcb4cac.

76. Chuck3. Emotional Intelligence in Agile. *Agile Project Management*. [Online] [Cited: 22 June 2018.] http://managedagile.com/emotional-intelligence-and-agile/.

77. Pittman, Art. EQ for an Agile IT. *Inner Joining.* [Online] [Cited: 18 May 2018.] http://www.innerjoining.com/eq-for-an-agile-it/.

78. What are T-shaped Skills? *HR Zone.* [Online] [Cited: 15 September 2019.] https://www.hrzone.com/hr-glossary/what-are-t-shaped-skills.

79. Anatomy of a T-Shaped Employee & How to Be One. *Office Ninjas.* [Online] [Cited: 11 August 2019.] https://officeninjas.com/what-makes-t-shaped-employees-at-work/.

80. The Generalized Specialist: How Shakespeare, Da Vinci, and Kepler Excelled. *Farnam Street.* [Online] [Cited: 28 August 2019.] https://fs.blog/2017/11/generalized-specialist/.

81. Schneider, William E. *The Reengineering Alternative: A Plan for Making Your Current Culture Work.* Unknown : McGraw-Hill, 1999.

82. Salesforce.com. Is Poor Collaboration Killing Your Company? *Salesforce.com.* [Online] 12 September 2012. [Cited: 21 April 2018.] https://www.salesforce.com/blog/2012/09/nick-stein-work-post-2.html.

83. Francino, Yvette. What is collaboration and why is it important to Agile methodologies? *SearchQualitySoftware*. [Online] TechTarget. [Cited: 25 May 2018.] https://searchsoftwarequality.techtarget.com/answer/What-is-collaboration-and-why-is-it-important-to-Agile-methodologies.

84. Yeates, Clancy. ANZ Bank restructure to create '150 start-ups'. *The Sydney Morning Herald*. [Online] 10 September 2017. [Cited: 30 June 2018.] https://www.smh.com.au/business/banking-and-finance/anz-bank-restructure-to-create-150-startups-20170906-gybxr8.html.

85. Frost, James. ANZ gets serious about agile management with new way of working. *Australian Financial Review*. [Online] 31 January 2018. [Cited: 2 July 2018.] https://www.afr.com/business/banking-and-finance/financial-services/anz-gets-serious-about-agile-management-with-new-way-of-working-20180130-h0qnrm+&cd=2&hl=en&ct=clnk&gl=au.

86. Barska, Emilia. Spotify Engineering Model with Squads, Tribes, Chapters and Guilds. *Growly.io*. [Online] 8 March 2017. [Cited: 20 April 2018.] https://www.growly.io/spotify-engineering-model-with-squads-tribes-chapters-and-guilds/.

87. Layton, Mark C. Applying Agile Management Value 3: Customer Collaboration Over Contract Negotiation. *Dummies*. [Online] [Cited: 3 March 2018.] https://www.dummies.com/careers/project-management/applying-agile-management-value-3-customer-collaboration-over-contract-negotiation/.

88. Relevance's Perspective on Agile Methods. *Relevance.* [Online] [Cited: 25 June 2018.] http://thinkrelevance.com/how-we-work/agile_principles.

89. Servant Leadership. *Wikipedia.* [Online] [Cited: 1 July 2018.] https://en.wikipedia.org/wiki/Servant_leadership.

90. Greenleaf, Robert K. What is Servant Leadership? *Greenleaf Center for Servant Leadership.* [Online] [Cited: 13 June 2018.] https://www.greenleaf.org/what-is-servant-leadership/.

91. Sinek, Simon. *Leaders Eat Last.* Unkown : Portfolio, 2017. 978-0670923175.

92. How the All Blacks started a trend sweeping the sporting world. *The New Daily.* [Online] 11 September 2017. [Cited: 3 August 2019.] https://thenewdaily.com.au/sport/union/2017/09/11/all-blacks/.

93. What Is a Self-Organizing Team? *PlanView.* [Online] [Cited: 20 February 2019.] https://www.planview.com/resources/articles/what-is-self-organizing-team/.

94. THE NEXT GENERATION Working Life - Ericsson. *Ericsson.* [Online] [Cited: 16 August 2019.] https://www.ericsson.com/assets/local/news/2014/2/ericsson-working-life-survival-guide.pdf.

95. *The power and illusion of self-organizing teams.* Juli, Thomas. Vancouver, British Columbia, Canada : Project Management Institute, 2012.

96. Cohn, Mike. The Role of Leaders on a Self-Organizing Team. *Mountain Goat Software*. [Online] 7 January 2010. [Cited: 4 February 2018.] https://www.mountaingoatsoftware.com/blog/the-role-of-leaders-on-a-self-organizing-team.

97. Clippinger, John Henry III. *The Biology of Business*. s.l. : Jossey-Bass, 1999. ISBN-13: 978-0787943240.

98. Keller, Scott and Meaney, Mary. High-performing teams: A timeless leadership topic. *McKinsey Quarterly*. June, 2017.

99. Wiese, Carl and Ricci, Ron. *The Collaboration Imperative: Executive Strategies for Unlocking Your Organization's True Potential*. s.l. : Cisco Systems, 2011. ISBN-13: 978-0983941705.

100. Luyten, Stephan. Tuckman in an agile world: How scrum facilitates a fast evolution to a performing team. *Medium*. [Online] 7 August 2014. [Cited: 15 May 2018.] https://medium.com/@stefanluyten/tuckman-in-an-agile-world-e1d92ebfb4d2.

101. Miller, Talan. When four worlds colide. *Training Journal*. [Online] May 2014. [Cited: 13 June 2018.] http://www.belbin.com/media/1397/when-4-worlds-collide-tj-2014.pdf.

102. Webster, Vicky and Webster, Martin. What Everybody Ought to Know About Team Building and Situational Leadership. *Leadership Thoughts*. [Online] [Cited: 27 June 2018.] https://www.leadershipthoughts.com/team-building-and-situational-leadership/.

103. Duhigg, Charles. What Google learnbed from its quest to build the perfect team. *New York Times*. [Online] 25 February 2016. [Cited: 27 March 2018.] https://www.nytimes.com/2016/02/28/magazine/what-google-learned-from-its-quest-to-build-the-perfect-team.html.

104. *Earned value management systems (EVMS)*. Reichel, Chance W. Seattle, WA : Project Management Institute, 2006.

105. Lee, JongSun. Earned value management systems key document integration using Excel. *Project Management Institute*. [Online] Project Management Institute, 26 October 2014. [Cited: 13 March 2019.] https://www.pmi.org/learning/library/earned-value-management-systems-document-integration-excel-9284.

106. Widman, Jake. IT's biggest project failures -- and what we can learn from them. *Computerworld*. [Online] 9 October 2008. [Cited: 3 July 2018.] https://www.computerworld.com/article/2533563/it-project-management/it-s-biggest-project-failures----and-what-we-can-learn-from-them.html.

107. Nieto-Rodriguez, Antonio. Notorious project failures -- Berlin airport: Why did it go wrong? *CIO*. [Online] 24 April 2017. [Cited: 11 May 2018.] https://www.cio.com/article/3185909/project-management/notorious-project-failures-berlin-airport-why-did-it-go-wrong.html.

108. Liker, Jeffrey. *The Toyota Way: 14 Management Principles From the World's Greatest Manufacturer*. s.l. : Mhe Us, 2003. ISBN-13: 978-0071392310.

109. Millard, Maggie. Everyday Examples of the 8 Wastes of Lean. *KaiNexus Blog*. [Online] 13 July 2016. [Cited: 5 June 2019.] https://blog.kainexus.com/improvement-disciplines/lean/7-wastes-of-lean/everyday-examples-of-the-8-wastes-of-lean.

110. Exceeding Value. *The Standish Group*. [Online] The Standish Group. [Cited: 16 March 2019.] https://www.standishgroup.com/sample_research_files/Exceeding%20Value_Layout.pdf.

111. Nottage, Suzanne. GO WITH THE FLOW: your Scrum teams are interrupted 2,000 times per sprint. Let's talk about flow. *Last Conference*. Sydney : s.n., 2019.

112. Sutil, Emiliano. My way to #noestimates. *LinkedIn*. [Online] 11 July 2019. [Cited: 17 September 2019.] https://www.linkedin.com/pulse/my-way-noestimates-emiliano-sutil/.

113. Li, Huimin. How estimating with "story counts" worked for us. *Thoughtworks website*. [Online] Thoughtworks. [Cited: 9 September 2019.] https://www.thoughtworks.com/insights/blog/how-estimating-story-counts-worked-us.

114. Popova, Albina. Putting #noestimates in action. *Medium*. [Online] 1 November 2016. [Cited: 12 December 2018.] https://tech.xing.com/putting-noestimates-in-action-2dd389e716dd.

115. Seiden, Joshua. *Outcomes Over Output - JS in his book Outcomes over Outputs defines*. s.l. : Sense & Respond Press, 2019. JS in his book Outcomes over Outputs defines .

116. Linders, Ben. Using Cost of Delay to Quantify Value and Urgency. *InfoQ.* [Online] 6 February 2015. [Cited: 22 July 2018.] https://www.infoq.com/news/2015/02/cost-of-delay/.

117. Andreasson, Ingemar. Getting flow into your product development. *Lean Magazine.* [Online] Softhouse , 11 April 2011. [Cited: 12 September 2019.] http://leanmagazine.net/issues/issue-6/getting-flow-into-your-product-development/.

118. Snowded. File:Cynefin as of 1st June 2014.png. *Wikipedia.* [Online] 6 July 2014. [Cited: 3 August 2017.] https://commons.wikimedia.org/w/index.php?curid=33783436.

119. The Economist. The creed of speed. *The Economist.* [Online] 5 December 2015. [Cited: 19 August 2017.] https://www.economist.com/briefing/2015/12/05/the-creed-of-speed.

120. Tobak, Steve. Why 'Fail Fast, Fail Often' Is All Hype. *Entrepreneur.* [Online] 25 January 2017. [Cited: 3 March 2018.] https://www.entrepreneur.com/article/288147.

121. Pixton, Pollyanna. Where Is the Learning in Agile? *Dr Dobbs.* [Online] 27 May 2014. http://www.drdobbs.com/architecture-and-design/where-is-the-learning-in-agile/240168308.

122. *Trust--the key for successful delivery using agile methods.* Petrén, Mattias Georgson. Marsailles, France. : PMI® Global Congress 2012—EMEA, 2012.

Notes

[1] Permission for reuse granted by Harvard Business Review on April 27, 2020.

[2] Reproduced with permission from Ahmed Sidky, Riot Games and ICAgile.

[3] Dave Snowden, released under CC BY-SA 3.0.

[4] Reproduced with permission from Karn G. Bulsuk.

[5] Reproduced from Wikipedia under CC BY-SA 3.0.

[6] Permission for re-use provided by Ken Rubin of Innolution.

www.ingramcontent.com/pod-product-compliance
Lightning Source LLC
Chambersburg PA
CBHW071545200326
41519CB00021BB/6615